AN INTRODUCTION TO BUSINESS PROFESSIONAL SKILS

B.COM/BBA

SREELAKSHMI ANAND

Made with ♥ on the Notion Press Platform
www.notionpress.com

Contents

Preface

Dear Students,

Welcome to "An Introduction to Business Professional Skills" for B.com/BBA Students, this book is written to increase student access to high-quality learning materials, maintaining the highest standards of academic rigor at little to no cost.

Business Professional Skills constitute a core component of the B.com/BBA degree courses. It is the base for their future education.

This book attempts to help the students by providing good notes & explanations by reducing their confusion. This book ensures the students that they will secure good marks for the examination.

Regards,

Sreelakshmi Anand

M.com (Finance)

Assistant Professor in Commerce

Sree Narayana Education Society College, Calicut

sreelakshmianand37@gmail.com

CHAPTER ONE

Professionalism

What is a Profession?

- A paid Occupation founded upon specialized education and training
- It is a type of work that needs a high level of formal education skills and training
- Examples of the profession are: Teaching, Medicine, Engineering, Accounting, etc

Characteristics of Profession

- It is based on specialized knowledge and skill
- It is acquired through prolonged formal education
- It demands practical training in the area
- It renders a specialized social service
- It is bound by a distinctive ethical code and standard of behavior
- Existence of professional organization

Who is a professional?

- A professional is a member of a profession who earns their living from a specified professional activity
- A professional is a person who acquires specialized knowledge and skill through formal education and training

Professionalism

- It is the conduct, behavior, and attitude of someone in a work or business environment
- It is competence or skill expected from a professional
- It is the way one conducts work in a positive way
- It also includes the way a manager or employee interacts with each other people in the organization
- According to Eric Mochnacz " Professionalism is someone's inherent ability to do what is expected of them and deliver quality work because they are driven to do so"

Characteristics of Professionalism (Qualities of a Good Professional)

- Specialized knowledge – Acquired through formal education
- Skills(Technical & Soft Skills)
- Competency – Capability to apply the knowledge and skill in the area
- Self-confidence
- Commitment
- Responsible Behaviour
- Appearance

- Reliability
- Code of ethics
- Positive attitude
- Continuous learning
- Hard work
- Proper demeanor and well organized

Professionalism in Business

- Professionalism is necessary for the long term success of every business whether it's a big corporation or not
- It does not mean just wearing a suit, leading a team, or obtaining an advanced academic degree. It entails expressing the values of responsibility, integrity, excellence, and accountability at all times
- A manager who works professionally can encourage employees to work with loyalty and commitment
- A professional work attitude and appearance allows employees to take pride in their work and improve working performance
- relationships with employees, customers, and other stakeholders are of vital importance to ensure that company goals and objectives are met.
- Professionalism is required in the following areas :

  1) Working environment
  2) Management of business
  3) Employee & customer interaction etc

Need and Importance of Professionalism in Business

- Encourage personal improvement

- Establishes respect and appropriate boundaries
- Promotes & maintains accountability
- Establishes a good culture
- Communication effectiveness
- Minimizes conflicts
- Helps to achieve mission & objectives
- Enhances advancement &growth of business
- Business reputation & positive brand Association

Professional Skills Required in Business

- Professional skills are the skills& competencies required for every professional. These skills depend upon the nature of the business or profession. These can be classified into a) Personal skills or soft skills b)Technical skills or Hard skills c) Hybrid skills (Combination of both soft and hard skills)

1. **Personal Skills or Soft Skills**

- Soft skills are the personal attributes, personality traits & inherent cues needed for success in life and business
- These are intangible skills that help a person to interact and get along well with others
- These are the skills required for every individual in a business
- It consists of interpersonal skills and interpersonal skills

Intra Personal Skills

- Creativity: Skills to generate & develop new ideas
- Enthusiasm: Lively interested in something
- Confidence: Trust in own abilities

- Honesty & Integrity: Quality of being honest, reliable & consistent
- Positive attitude: Optimistic & hopeful about situations
- Common sense: Sound practical judgment based on the perception of situations & facts
- Flexibility: Willingness to change according to situations
- Time Management: Divide available time between specific activities & control
- Self-control & Emotional stability : ability to control emotions &remain stable under difficult situations

Inter-Personal Skills

- Friendliness: Quality of behaving in a pleasant & kind way towards someone.
- Good Manners: Consider the feeling of other people during interactions.
- Listening Skills: Ability to receive & interpret messages & to focus completely on the speaker.
- Empathy: Ability to understand & share feelings of another as oneself.
- Communication Skills: Ability to convey information through verbal & nonverbal means.
- Leadership Skills: Ability to motivate & lead people to act towards a common goal.
- Stress Management Skills: Ability to control a person's stress level.
- Team Work: Ability to work collectively as a group.
- Public Speaking Skill: Ability to address & communicate well with a large group
- Decision-Making Skill: Ability to choose the right & best among available options.

- Organization Skills: Ability to organize people & objects creating a structure & order for everything.
- Problem Solving Skills: Ability to determine the source of the problem, analyze & find an effective solution.
- Planning & Controlling: Ability to plan everything & execute the plan in a successful manner

1.
Technical Skills or Hard Skills

- These are specific capabilities to perform particular jobs. These abilities & Knowledge are learned through education or training. These are also known as job-specific skills because the technical skills required for business may vary according to the nature & structure of business in business.

Technical Skills used in Business

- Computer Skills
- Reporting Skills
- Finance & Accounting Skills
- Marketing Skills
- Management Skill
- Hard Communication Skill
- Data Analysis Skill
- Machine Operate & Maintain Skill
- Skill in Network structure & Securities

Professionalism in Communication

What is communication?

Communication is the process of exchanging information between individuals through verbal & non-verbal means. It is the process of sending & receiving messages that conveys information, ideas, thoughts, feelings & emotions. Communication is very important in personal life & workplace. A communication process shall consist of Sender, Receiver, Message, and Channel & Feedback

- It refers to communication in the business profession or workplace.
- It encompasses written, oral, visual & digital communication within a workplace context.
- It is the interaction made between co-workers, customers, supervisors & other outside parties of business.
- The purpose of professional communication is to Inform, Persuade, Instruct, and Request & Respond to requests.

Types of Professional Communication

Non-Verbal Communication

- It is the transmission of messages or signals through non-verbal platforms such as eye contact, facial expressions & posture.
- It is used for both formal & informal communication.
- It improves a person's ability to relate, engage & establish meaningful interactions.
- It improves the efficiency of oral communication.

Verbal Communication

- It is the use of words to share information with other people.
- It includes both spoken & written communication.
- It may be formal or informal communication.
- It includes both manual & digital communication.

Oral - Staff Meeting, Business Letter, Telephone Conversation, Interviews

Written - Interviews, Business Memo (Memorandum), Email & Voice mail, Public Presentation, Notice

Digital - Vlogging & Blogging, Personal discussion, Minutes(Written record of decisions), Social Networking, Circular(Official letter with instructions) & Report, Video Conferencing

Importance of Verbal Communication

- It is the most important media for formal & official communication in business.
- It serves as a record of references.
- It helps to clarify misunderstandings.
- It is helpful to maintain successful business relationships.
- It helps to build a positive image of the organization.
- It improves efficiency & productivity.

Professional Presentation

- Professional Communication is the oral presentation or speech delivered to a live audience such as **Employees, Customers, Shareholders,** etc.
- It may be online or offline. Creating an effective presentation is an important skill for professionals.
- Each & every business presentation must be memorable & able to change the minds of the audience.

- The main purpose of the presentation is to give information & to persuade the audience to act on a particular matter.
- Business presentations must be organized well in advance.
- A good presentation should have good subject matter, match the objective, best fit the audience & should be well organized.

Organization of a Presentation

A good presentation should organize in the following manner:

I. **Greet the audience & introduce yourself**:
II. **Introduction**: Well planned, Time-bound, with eye-catching techniques.
III. **Body**: Well organized with supporting materials & aids.
IV. **Summary**: Brief replication of entire presentation.
V. **Discussion**: Question & answer session after the presentation.
VI. **Conclusion**: Conclusion after discussion.
VII. **Thanking the audience**

Requisites of a Good Presentation:

i. **Include a goal/objective before the presentation.**
ii. **Right Content**: Structured & logically organized content
iii. **Organized Matter**: Organize the content into introduction, body, summary & conclusion
iv. **Concise & Focused on the topic**
v. **Good appearance & Posture**
vi. **Good Communication Skills**: Verbal & Non-verbal Communication.
vii. **Avoid common mistakes.**
viii. **Use of supporting materials**: Such as documents, pictures, examples, quotations & videos

ix. **Eye contact in offline presentations.**
x. **Time management**
xi. **Encourage questions from the audience**
xii. **Summarize the presentation at the end**
xiii. **Discussion session at the end**
xiv. **Feedback & Follow up**

Common Mistakes to be avoided in Presentations

- No planning & Research
- Poor Content
- Reading Speech & at n appropriate time for the audience
- Bad body language & failure to make eye contact
- Lack of conviction
- Not enough audiovisuals & Not using the legible font in slides
- Too much slide on a text(too small to read)
- Technical problems like power failure, loss of connectivity, etc.
- No discussions, feedback & follow up

Different Presentation Postures

- **Standing**: Standing up straight, relaxed, stand with feet apart & shoulders squared, facing the audience.
- **Hands & Arms**: Keep hands between shoulders & hips, move hands according to speech, do not place hands in pocket, and do not fold hands.
- **Eye Contact**: Look at the audience, rotate eye contact, and don't look down or at the material.
- **Head**: Hold head high with a smile, not to fidget.
- **Body movements**: Appropriate to the speech

- **Palm up & Palm down**: Palm up indicates openness & honesty and Palm down indicates a sign of strength & authority.
- **Steeple the hands**: Gives confidence to some speakers
- **Rotate or change positions**: Do not maintain the same positions thought a presentation.
- **Opened & Closed Posture**:
- **Mirroring**: Mirroring is the behavior in which one person unconsciously imitates the gestures, speech pattern, or attitude of another.

Written Communication:

- Written communication involves any type of interaction that makes use of the written word.
- The written communication is the most common and effective mode of business communication.
- In any organization, electronic mails, memos, reports, documents, letters, journals, job descriptions, employee manuals, etc. are some of the commonly used forms of written communication.

Important Written Communication in Business:

- **Business Letters**: Printed letters sent by mail, speed post, courier, etc. It is generally used for external communication.
- **Email (Electronic Mail)**: It is a message or letter sent via the internet. It helps to connect people inside & outside the business.
- **Business Memo (Memorandum)**: Short document used to transmit official information within a business organization.

- **Notice**: It is a written or printed announcement to inform a large number of people about something in the business.
- **Circular**: It is an official letter containing some important information, instruction, or orders distributed to many people. It is used for internal communication.
- **Reports**: A document prepared to communicate the outcome of an activity or assigned job. It is used for internal & external reporting.
- **Agenda & Minutes**: The agenda is the outline of the topics that must be taken up during a meeting. Minutes are the written records of the decision taken in a meeting.
- **Promotional Materials**: It consists of catalogs, Leaflets, Press Reports, Brochures, Business Cards, Advertising material, etc.
- **Employee manuals**: It is a handbook given to employees. It contains job-related information that employees need to know.
- **Other Documents**: Resolutions, Questionnaires, Survey Reports, Research Reports, Memorandum & Articles, etc.

Benefits/ Merits of Written Communication:

- Legal Document
- Formal & Authoritative
- Creates permanent Record
- Accurate & Precise
- Suitable for long-distance communication
- Clear & Complete understanding
- Suitable for long messages
- Less possibility for distortion
- It is best suitable for standing orders & reports
- Suitable for sending statistical data
- It can be sent to many persons
- Build goodwill & image

Limitations/ Demerits of Written Communication:

- It is time-consuming
- It is expensive
- No secrecy
- No instant clarification & feedback
- Less flexibility
- Not suitable for emergency
- Not suitable for an illiterate person
- Lack of personal touch

Technical Documents in Business:

- Technical documents refer to any document that explains the use, functionality, creation, or architecture of a product or process in business.
- Technical documents include a wide range of documents used to inform or persuade a target audience with a specific need.
- Technical documents provide information about the underlying architecture of the product, how to install it, how to operate it etc.
- It includes end-user documents, operation & installation manuals, marketing communications, training materials, technical reports, etc.
- Examples: User manual of the product, installation guide of a product

Types of technical documents in Business:

- **User Manual (User Guide)**: A user manual is a technical communication document intended to assist people on how to use a product.
- **Installation Guide**: It is a type of technical document that describes the steps required to install software & hardware elements of a product that requires to be assembled.
- **API Document**: An API (Application Programming Interface) is a software intermediary that allows two applications to communicate with each other. API provides all information & instructions required to work with API.
- **Release Note**: These are technical documents distributed with software products that contain bug fixes & added features
- **System Description Document**: It is a document that describes what the system will do & what are services offered.
- **Market Requirements Document (MRD)**: It is a technical document that expresses the customer's wants & needs for the product or service. It usually explains who the target audience is what products compete with this one, and why customers are likely to want this product.
- **Other Reports**:

i. Annual reports of companies
ii. Feasibility study reports
iii. Project reports
iv. Technical guides & handbooks
v. Warranty cards & Research reports
vi. Business plans
vii. Newsletters & Webpages
viii. Brochure & catalogues

Technical Documentation (Technical Writing):

- It is the process of writing technical documents in business.

- It is a practice of writing, preparing & processing technical documents.
- The process includes the determination of document standards & the preparation of documents as per the prescribed standard.
- The purpose of technical writing is to provide material that explains a process or makes a complex concept easier to understand for a particular audience.

Technical Writing Standards:

- Technical writing standards are the principles, rules, guidelines & norms to be followed while writing technical documents.
- They provide guidelines on what contents to include, the writing style & the layout of the document.
- These standards depend upon the industry, nature of the product, user requirements, etc.

Universal Principles/Standards of Technical Writing:

- **Quality content**: The content of the document must be complete & comprehensive.
- **Coherent**: There must be a logical association between parts of the content.
- **Clarity in Communication**: The document should convey the intended message without ambiguity.
- **Accuracy**: It should provide correct & error-free information.
- **Understand Purpose**: It should be prepared for the document.
- **Understand the User**: It should be drafted by the requirement of the end-user.
- **Accessibility**: It should be attractive & accessible. Documents shall include proper header, footers, navigation tools, etc.

- **Simple Language & Proper Care on Grammar**: It should be prepared in simple language & proper care should be given to spelling & grammar.
- **Consistent**: Maintain one style & format throughout the document.
- **Concise**: It shall contain only relevant information.
- **Table of Contents**: Good table of contents &indexing helps the user to find the required matter from the documents easily.
- **Avoid Jargon**: Avoid industry-specific words that are difficult for others to understand.

Electronic Mail (E-mail)

- It is an electronic message that can be sent from one computer to another by using a network such as an internet.
- It is one of the most widely used features of the internet.
- Through email, users can communicate quickly & easily with millions of people around the world at any time.
- It is the cheapest & fastest communication medium.
- Documents, Pictures, Audio, Video, etc. can be attached to the email.
- Messages are sent from one E-mail address (ID) to another (ID).
- An email id is a series of characters made up of :

- Username
- @ Symbol
- Name of user's ISP
- Domain name

Eg: xyzcompany@gmail.com

https://docs.google.com/forms/d/1ZAtv12mwTq3SI8P0Ov_8dSFi1GpQiAC1q4rAL-rli0o/edit?usp=sharing

Popular Email Service Providers

- **Gmail**: By Google
- **Outlook**: By Microsoft
- **iCloud Mail**: By Apple
- **Yahoo Mail**: 1 TB free Storage
- **Proton Mail**: Open-source & secure service provider with unlimited storage.
- **AOL Mail**: Oldest web mail service provider with unlimited storage.
- **Rediff Mail**: One of the oldest service provider

Common Email Terms

- **Inbox**: It is the folder or repository where incoming messages to the mail ID are stored.
- **Compose**: It is the option to create a new message to save or send.
- **Spam (Junk mail)**: Unsolicited & unwanted messages such as marketing messages, advertisements, etc.
- **Phishing email**: It is a cybercrime used to gather personal information such as user name, password, debit or credit card details, etc. through email, SMS, telephone calls, etc. Private data captured through an email designed to look like a trusted third party is called a Phishing email.
- **Cc (Carbon Copy)**: It is the line to write the list of co-recipients in the case of multiple receivers. Recipients can see the list of all recipients.
- **Bcc (Blinded Carbon Copy)**: It is also the line to write the list of co-recipients but, recipients cannot see the list of other recipients.

Features of Email

v. It is an electronic message sent from one electronic device to another.
v. Automatic reply to messages is possible.
v. Webmail & mobile email apps can be used to receive & send messages.
v. E-mail can attach files- Documents, Audio, Video, Compressed folders, Pictures, etc.
v. There is an attachment limit for different service providers.
v. Multi forward facility: It allows us a facility to send copies of a message to many people.
v. Addresses can be stored in an address book & retrieved instantly.
v. Signatures can be attached automatically.
v. Notification if a message cannot be delivered
v. Emails are automatically dated & time stamped.
v. Facility to get notifications or reminders on important mails.
v. The recipient can open the mailbox & read the message at his convenience.
v. It provides free mailbox storage.
v. Email uses multiple protocols:

- SMTP (Simple Mail Transfer Protocol) is used to send messages.
- POP (Post Office Protocol) or IMAP (Internet Message Access Protocol) are used to retrieve messages from a mail server.

Advantages of Email:

- Helpful for internal & external communications.
- Cheap & fast communication medium

- Easy retrieval
- It is used as a marketing tool (Newsletters)
- Appointment with reminders
- Helps to schedule meetings
- Useful to share files
- Automated email messages

Disadvantages of Email

- Spam
- Internet & email security issues
- Sent mails cannot be deleted
- Limited size of attachments
- Limited free storage
- No regular checking
- Not suitable for internal communications, informal communications

Email Etiquette (Netiquette)

- It refers to the principles of behavior that one should follow when writing or answering email messages.
- It is the code of conduct for email communication.
- In business, it is the professionalism in using email.
- Email etiquette depends upon the receiver of the message.
- Different etiquettes are to be followed in business while sent to friends, relatives, partners, customers, employees, superiors & subordinates.

Email Etiquette Format

1. **To Line:** If the message is sent to one person, it is essential to use 'To'
2. **Cc Line:** If the email is sent to multiple recipients & the list of recipients is not confidential, use the Cc line to type the recipient address. Both the main recipient & co-recipient can see the mail address list.
3. **Bcc Line:** If the email is sent to multiple recipients & the list of recipients is confidential, use the Bcc line to type the recipient address. In this case, neither the main recipient nor the co-recipient can see the mail address list.
4. **Clear & Concise Subject Line:** Subject line must be short, precise, informative & convey the main point of the message
5. **Salutation:** Always begin business emails with a formal salutation comfortable to the sender.
6. **Content (Message):** Content must be clear, brief & well arranged. Long & badly structured sentences confuse the reader.
7. **Closing:** Complementary sentences such as 'Thank You, 'Best Wishes', 'Regards' etc. are to be used to conclude the message.
8. **Append Signature:** Append signature & address in proper format with all outgoing mails of business.
9. **Attachments:** It must be low in size (Compress large attachments), converted to common formats such as PDF, etc. & must be virus-free.

Email Etiquette Do's

- Use a professional email address while making business communications.
- Attention to spelling, grammar & capitalization.
- The tone in writing must be positive.

- Compliance with rules of the country- with regards to electronic communications & privacy.
- Newsletters must include a link to unsubscribe easily.
- Use standard fonts with legible font size.
- Double check you have selected the correct recipient & the email ID is correct.
- It is better to send different emails for different subjects. All subjects in one mail make the mail complex to read & understand.
- Read the message before sending it to ensure that it is proper & error-free. Add the email address last to ensure that it is not sent before finishing writing.
- Provide all supporting information & relevant attachments.
- Check inbox at regular intervals.
- Add disclaims in emails if necessary: to protect the company from liability.
- Think twice before clicking 'Reply All' – Ensure that everyone on the list needs to receive the email.
- Try to reply to emails even if the mail was not intended for you.

Email Etiquette Don'ts

- Avoid jokes, emojis, references to politics & religion, etc. in company mail.
- Avoid multiple subjects in one mail.
- Do not copy or reproduce a received message or attachment without the permission of the sender.
- Do not use emails for confidential information.
- Never respond if you are upset.
- Don't attach unnecessary files.
- Never send emails with all text in the capital.
- Do not use abbreviations in formal business communications.

CHAPTER TWO

Electronic Learning (E-Learning)

Electronic Learning (E-Learning)

- E-Learning is the learning conducted through electronic media.
- Electronic media consist of radio, television, smartphones, the internet, etc.
- It is a learning system utilizing electronic technologies to access educational materials.
- It is the use of technology that enables people to learn anything, anywhere, and anytime.
- Today e-learning is mostly conducted through the internet.

Examples of e-Learning platforms/Tools

- Educational search engines such as Google scholar, Microsoft academic, Research Gate, etc.
- Online school classes through the kite victor's channel.
- Live online classes through Google meet, zoom, etc.
- Learning management systems (LMS) such as Microsoft team, Edmodo, Google classes, etc.

- YouTube Education Videos & Live stream classes.

Characteristics of e-Learning

- It is a computer and internet-based educational system.
- It uses electronic media & information technology.
- It enables individuals to learn anything, anywhere, and anytime.
- It provides education to people of different ages and backgrounds.
- It promotes lifelong learning.
- Computer, smartphones, and the internet are the main component of e-learning.
- E-learning utilizes the educational materials available in different formats such as documents, e-books, audios, videos, slides, live classes, etc.
- It is used for formal, informal, and distance learning.
- It is also called online learning, virtual learning, web-based learning, etc.

Advantages of e-learning

- **Convenience:** It can be conducted on different platforms, in different forms, and at different times convenient to the users.
- **Anytime Accessibility:**It is accessible 24 hours a day and 7 days a week as per the convenience of the user.
- **Low Cost:** The cost of e-learning is comparatively low compared to physical learning.
- **Addresses Individual Learner's Differences:** It can be specifically designed to address the needs of different learners.
- **Flexibility:**e-learning is flexible in terms of time and place of learning.

- **Anonymity**: Learners can participate in the learning process without disclosing /her identity. It is beneficial for shy students.
- **Encourages Interactions:**e-learning facilitates increased student-teacher interactions.
- **Repeated Learning**: online lectures and recorded videos can be seen any number of times
- **Access to Update Content:** Online materials are comprehensive and up-to-date.
- **Less Impact on Environment:** It is paperless, uses less power, avoids deforestation, etc.
- **Best Suitable for Part-Time & Distance Learning:** It is useful for those who don't have access to the formal education system.
- **Variety of Resources:** It can take a variety of resources such as text, audio, video, animations, graphics, multi-media, etc.

Drawbacks of E-learning

- **Technical Issues:** Lossof connectivity, failure of electronic equipment power failure, etc., may affect e-learning.
- **Poor Assessment Capability:** Most of the online assessments are limited to questions that are only objective. There are chances for malpractices in online tests.
- **Not Suitable for All Subjects:** It may not be suitable for practical-based papers and problem papers. It is suitable for social sciences but not for medicine and engineering which require hands-on practical training.
- **Health Problems:** Excessive use of computers, mobile phones, and the internet may create health issues such as eye strain, back pain, sleeping disorders, psychological issues, etc.
- **Limited Scope of Interactions and Feedback:** Most online learning platforms lack deep interaction between the participants. Immediate face-to-face feedback may not be possible on all online platforms.

- **Plagiarism:** Plagiarism is the practice of taking or copying the work of others without permission or citation. Online materials may contain illegally copied content.
- **It Requires Strong Self-Motivation And Time Management:** Lack of self-motivation, lack of time management, the influence of external factors, etc., may affect e-learning.
- **Digital Divide:** e-learning is in-accessible to computer illiterate people. People with less computer knowledge may also struggle with e-learning media and content.
- **Lack of Personal Touch:** It lacks the personal touch that helps learners move beyond their difficulties.
- **Feel of Isolation:** Online learning is a solo act and the learner may feel a sense of isolation.

Principles for effective and successful e-learning

- **Match to the Curriculum:** It should be suitable to the curriculum and its objective.
- **Inclusion:** It must be able to include all categories of learners including the physically or mentally disabled.
- **Learner Engagement:**Learners should be motivated to engage in the learning process.
- **Innovative Approaches:** Innovative technology, new online education tools, etc., is to be used in e-learning.
- **Effective Learning:**The content and methods of online education must be suitable to the needs of the learner.
- **Formative Assessment:**Regular assessment should be conducted along with the teaching-learning process.
- **Summative Assessment:** An online test may be conducted at the end of the learning process to understand the level of learner achievement.
- **Coherence, Consistency, and Transparency:**The pedagogy and it's the content must be logical, consistent, and clear.

- **Ease of Use:**Methods and techniques used for e-learning must be easy to use by the learner.
- **Cost Effectiveness:** The cost of technology solutions must be affordable to the learner.

Major technologies used in e-learning

- **Search Engines &Educational Search Engines:** Search engines such as Google, yahoo can be used. Educational search engines such as Google scholar, research gate, etc., can be used to search for specific e-learning materials on the net.

- **Blogging And Vlogging:** A blog is a discussion site published on the web. Vlog is a platform used to share small videos. Both blogs and vlogs are now used for e-learning.

- **Mobile Devices With Wireless Connectivity:** Mobile devices such as laptops, tablets, mobile phones, etc can be used to access online educational content.

- **Augmented Reality:** Augmented reality(AR) is the real-time use of information in the form of text, graphics, audio, video, etc., integrated with real-world objects. It is the software applications that provide digital visual content similar to real-world situations. It can be best used for education and learning purposes.

- **Screen Casting:** A screencast is a digital recording of a computer screen. Screen-casting is now used to convert slides and other materials into video lessons. Examples, MS PowerPoint slide recorder, AZ screen recorder, free cam

- **Artificial Intelligence:** It is the intelligence demonstrated by machines similar to human intelligence. Intelligent software designed to cater to the individual needs of the students can be used in the e-learning process.

- **Learning Management Systems (LMS):** It is a software application used to manage the entire learning process. Modern LMS enables to schedule classes, conduct live streaming, mark attendance, management of assignments, conduct tests, etc. example Microsoft teams, moodle.

- **Internet Of Things (IoT):** IoT refers to the billions of physical devices around the world that are now connected to the internet, all collecting and sharing data. IoT devices give students better access to everything from learning materials to communication channels. It gives teachers the ability to measure student learning progress in real-time.

- **Cloud Computing:** It is the practice of using internet servers rather than physical devices to store, manage and process data. E-learning processes usually require many hardware and software resources and cloud computing can be used to replace these physical resources.

- **Video Platforms:** Several free video platforms are now available to publish And share educational videos. For example, Netflix, Vimeo, etc.

- **Virtual Laboratories:** A virtual laboratory is an on-screen simulator or calculator that learners use to test ideas and observed results. The learners can conduct experiments through this simulator equipment that behaves in almost the same way as it would be in a real environment. Examples of virtual science lab apps are project Noah, prop magic, etc.

- **Video Conferencing Applications:**

- Video conferencing applications such as zoom, Google meet, etc., can be used to conduct live classes.

Modes of Education

- **Based on the mode of delivery and administration, education may be classified into**

- **Traditional education**(conventional education):

Education is provided through lectures in regular classroom settings.

- **Online education:**

It is the education provided through the internet.

- **Hybrid education:**

It is education that combines face-to-face classroom instructions with online activities.

Online education

- Online education simply means the education delivered and administered through the internet
- It is the delivery of educational content and instruction via the internet to the students using home computers and smartphones.

- Khan defined online education as "the delivery of instructions to a remote audience using the web as an intermediary".
- Even though formal education in India still constitutes the traditional model, online education is evolving at a quick pace.

Features of online education

- It is the education delivered through the internet.
- It is the use of information and communication technology in education.
- Focus shifted from teaching to learning
- Online education facilities online learning.
- Online education is student-centered.
- It utilizes a variety of learning platforms.

Why online education? (Importance of online education)

- It is convenient for the user.
- It can be accessible at any time.
- it addresses individual learners' differences.
- Learners can participate without revealing their identity.
- Useful for part-time and distance education.
- It encourages interaction between teacher and student.
- It is flexible.
- Cost of education is low.
- Repeated learning possible.
- It is environment-friendly education.
- It can be used for formal, informal, and distance education.

Role of a teacher in online education

- **Developer of course materials**: one of the most important responsibilities of the teacher is the design and development of course materials in electronic format. It takes much more time than traditional education.
- **Guide and motivator**: online teacher has to play the role of a guide and should motivate the students to actively participate in the learning process.
- **Tech-savvy**: Teachers must be proficient in the use of modern technology, especially computers, the internet, and learning platforms.
- **Effective communicator**: online communication is different from traditional classroom communication. The online teacher must be able to manage all online communication media and techniques effectively.
- **Moderator and facilitator**: In that traditional classroom, the teacher has to play a moderator facilitating the interaction between learners.
- **Co-learner:** the online teacher must be a lifelong learner not only of course content but also of methods of online teaching.
- **Assessment**: teachers are responsible for making an assessment. Both formative and summative assessments may be employed to check the level of achievement of the learner.
- **Online individual support**: teacher is responsible to clarify the queries raised by the respondents during and after the instructional time.

Digital age learner

- We all live in the digital age or information age.

- A digital age learner is someone who utilizes digital technology for learning.
- All learners utilizing the online educational resources are called digital age learners.
- They are technology-savvy students or digital literates.
- Digital age learner knows how to navigate and find the appropriate educational content from the web.

Characteristics of digital age learners

- Busy with other works or employment
- Learning from home and work environment.
- Impatient-they want to get information fast with minimum effort.
- Digital natives, digital literates, and tech-savvy-they have grown up with digital technologies. They have knowledge and skill in using technology.
- Utilize different technologies to access knowledge-using mobile devices, advanced software, apps, etc.
- active in social media such as what's app, Facebook, and Twitter.
- Self-motivated to learn.

Role of the learner in online education

- **Tech-savvy**: he must be computer literate. He must have operational competencies to use ICT tools for learning.
- **Collaborative competencies**: he must be competent to communicate well online with teachers and co-learners.
- **Self-motivated and self-directing**: he must be ready to participate in the learning process voluntarily.

- **Willing to commit time**: he must be willing to commit sufficient time to his studies.
- **Critical thinker**: he must have abilities to think rationally and logically.
- **Participate in the assessment process**: he must undergo a regular assessment by the teacher or through an online quiz.

Approaches in Online Education (Approaches for E-Learning Delivery)

- **Self-paced and instructor-led:**

1. In self-placed learning, the learners initiate and direct their learning process. It is voluntary learning through online mode.
2. Instructor: led learning is the learning initiated and facilitated by a teacher or instructor. The learning environment is purposefully created.

- **Synchronous and asynchronous learning:**

1. synchronous learning occurs in real-time with the live interaction of all participants. Eg: online classes through Google meet or zoom.

2. In asynchronous learning, students learn pre-recorded or pre-written materials at different times and locations. Eg: learning through YouTube recorded classes.

- **Linear and nonlinear learning:**

1. Linear learning is the directed, controlled, and program-centered approach. The learner has to complete a certain level of content before moving to the next one. Eg: online courses with specific modules.

2. Nonlinear is a flexible approach to learning. Learners are provided with a variety of options and they can choose their path. There are no particular sequences of the learning process. eg: learning through assignments.

- **Individual and collaborative learning:**

1. Individual learning is self-learning or individualized instructions by the teacher. In individual learning, there is no scope for interactions with other learners.

2. Collaborative learning is a situation in which two or more people learn or attempt to learn something together. Students can socially interact with other students.

E-Learning as a service industry

- Service industry is an industry or business that creates and delivers services rather than tangible products.
- Since the education service is provided, e-learning can be considered a service industry.
- The e-learning industry in India is a productive one, witnessing a steady growth rate of around 25 percent year on year, and is projected to be a $1.96 billion industry by 2021.

- **E-learning and online education can be considered a service industry, because of the following reasons:**

- A specialized service is provided to society through online education.
- E-learning market consists of a large number of players working for profit.
- Most of the educational resources are directly and indirectly paid for.

- Companies are investing huge funds in the development of e-learning tools.
- Many traditional courses and training programs are replaced by online courses.
- Education sector contributes to the economic growth of the country.

E-learning in India (Online education in India)

- Till the end of the last century, the education system in India was working on traditional classroom-based learning.
- The concept of digital learning in India evolved at the beginning of the 21st century.
- Now the hybrid system of learning (both online and offline) is followed in India.

Key factors contributing to the growth of e-learning in India

- Rising demand from various segments.
- Growing number of smartphone users.
- Improving penetration of the internet.
- Digital India initiatives of the Government of India.
- Increasing participation at the Government level.
- Availability of free online platforms.

Challenges of e-learning in India

- Dominance of government sector which sticks to conventional learning.
- Majority of the population is living in rural areas where there is no sufficient infrastructure for e-learning.
- High digital divide-high gap between digital literates and illiterates.

- Lack of communication facilities.
- Slow internet connectivity.
- High cost of technology-cost of instruments and connectivity.

Internet-A knowledge repository

- Internet is a knowledge repository (database) that systematically stores information and knowledge.
- Internet resources can be easily tapped by any person who has taken the skills to Use of the internet.
- We can search for any kind of information on the net.
- Internet contains a good collection of e-knowledge resources such as online encyclopedias, e-books, and digital libraries.

Knowledge resources on the internet

1. **Electronics books (e-books):**

- Electronic book is a book available in a digital form readable on electronic devices such as computers, smartphones, and e-readers.
- It is the electronic version of the traditional printed book.
- Users can purchase an e-book on storage devices such as CD, but the most popular method of getting an e-book is to purchase a downloadable file of the e-book from the internet.
- Some e-books can be downloaded free of cost while others need to be purchased at a price.

There are three ways to read e-books:

- open and read e-books on electronic devices as other documents such as pdf files(not effective)
- read e-books in a physical e-book reader
- install an e-book reader software on your pc or mobile.

E-book reader

- An e-book reader is a portable handheld electronic device specialized for reading digital books.
- It enables readers to bookmark pages, make notes, highlight passages, check dictionaries, expand font, and save selected text.
- The e-book reader is normally designed to operate over long hours by consuming minimal power. eg: Amazon Kindle, Kobo, Sony reader.
- It is also available in the form of software or apps that can be installed on any device. eg: MS reader, kindle for pc, caliber, Amazon Kindle app, etc.

Features of e-book

1. **Digital form:** it is the electronic version of print books.
2. **Searchability:** reader can search for specific text in e-books.
3. **Referenceable:** e-book text contains links for reference or additional reading.
4. **Navigation**: reader can navigate to a specific page.
5. **Book mark**: reader can use electronic bookmarks to mark the area already read.
6. **Tangibility**: physical e-book readers make e-books tangible.

Advantages of e-books(overprinted books)

- E-books are delivered immediately after purchase. There are no packing and shipping expenses.
- It is accessible everywhere at any time.
- It is environment friendly (no paper, no tree-cutting needed).
- No need for large physical space(it can be stored in portable devices or on cloud storage.)
- Easy retrieval-stored e-books can be searched and retrieved easily.
- E-books are portable.
- E-books contain links for further information.
- E-books contain multi-media format(e-books can contain not only text and images, but also audio and even video).
- E-books are printable if necessary.
- E-books can be updated when a new edition is released.
- Fonts can be resized to meet the requirements of different users.
- the Same device can be used to read many books.
- Reading e-books via e-book readers enables the reader to bookmark pages, make notes, highlight passages, check dictionaries, adjust fonts, save selected text, etc.

Limitations of e-book

- Not convenient like printed books to read.
- E-books can cause eye strain.
- Reading e-books require power.
- Proper electronic devices such as e-book readers are needed for comfortable reading.
- E-book readers are costly.
- Publishers make restrictions on to use of e-books in libraries.

- Chance of piracy- there is a chance to share copyrighted books with others.
- Subject to internet threats-downloading e-books from the internet is subject to threats such as viruses, bugs, and other security issues.

Examples of free e-book repositories/digital libraries

1. BookBoon
2. Digilibraries
3. Feedbooks
4. Free-Ebook
5. Google books
6. Internet archive
7. Pdf book world
8. Wikibooks

2. Audio resources:

The following are the main audio resources on the internet that can be used for teaching and learning.

- Pronunciation of words-Eg. Pronunciation of a word in British and American English.
- Music in MP3 format musical training helps develop language and reasoning.
- Audio narration of text in visual presentations.
- Audio clips and lectures of renewed persons.

How to use audio in e-learning effectively?

- **Avoid text speech redundancies:** it should not be mere reading or narration of the text. It must be used to elaborate upon the subject.

- **Use audio with visuals:** for difficult topics to offer better understanding.
- **Use high-quality audio:** audio with high resolution and clarity.
- **Use standard and compatible audio formats:** such as MP3.
- **Audio instructions may be given:** for doing assignments, projects, etc.
- **Allow learners to control audio:** adjust volume, mute narration, record or save audio, etc.
- **Assess learner's knowledge:** learners are directed to develop and record audio presentations and to provide audio feedback.

3. <u>Video resources:</u>

- Video is the electronic medium for recording and displaying moving visuals with or without audio.
- Online and offline video resources can be best utilized for teaching and learning purposes.
- Teachers can use pre-recorded video classes or can interact with the learner through video conferencing tools.
- Number of free video-sharing platforms are available on the internet and the videos are now available in almost all subjects and languages

Video resources on the internet:

- Video hosting services: such as YouTube, Vimeo, Dailymotion, Flickr, etc.
- Educational video hosting services: such as Coursera, SchoolTube, mathTV, etc.
- Social media sites with video hosting: such as Facebook, Instagram, etc.
- Video search options in search engines:

- Video conferencing applications: such as Google meet&zoom.
- Learning management systems: with video hosting.

Benefits of using video in e-learning:

- Learning becomes more interesting.
- Keep the learners more engaged with the learning process.
- Easy understanding and retention.
- a Large amount of content can be presented in a limited time.
- Methods and procedures can be demonstrated easily.
- Complicated concepts can be described easily.
- Different learning styles can be accommodated.
- Encourage discussion.

How to use videos effectively in e-learning?

- Keep videos short.
- Video and sound quality must be good.
- Video size must be low and compressed for mobile viewing
- Add interactive elements
- Use appropriate color combinations.
- Use music and sound effects.
- Support video with additional learning materials or notes.
- Select appropriate video hosting platforms.

4. **Electronic journals:**

- It is a periodic publication in electronic format on the internet.
- It contains conceptual papers, research papers, review articles, etc.

- Free and paid platforms such as N LIST, science direct, STORE, etc., are available on the internet to access e-journals.

5. **Online encyclopedia (digital encyclopedia):**

- It is a huge online database that contains information on all branches of knowledge accessible through the internet.

6. **Online dictionary:**

- It is an online resource that lists the words of a language and gives their meaning, pronunciation, origin, usage, etc.
- Example: wiktionary, google dictionary, Macmillan dictionary.

7. **Web portals:**

- A web portal is a web-based platform that collects information that collects information from different sources and presents it uniformly. (eg: google, yahoo).
- It contains search engines, news, weather, email, calendar, etc.

8. **Other knowledge resources on the internet:**

- **New portals:** BBC world news, NDTV, etc.
- **Thesis reservoirs**: Shodhganga, OATD, etc.
- **Information websites:** provide a variety of information.
- **Blogs:** individual information web pages.
- **Newsgroups:** discussion forums on specific topics.eg, Usenet.
- **Question and answers websites:** such as quora &yahoo answers.

What is electronic content (E-content)?

- All content and information in digital format are called e-content.
- It is the content created and delivered through electronic media.
- It is the content or information in an electronic format that is delivered over a computer network such as the internet.
- E-content is available in all subjects and almost all levels of education.
- E-content has become a valuable and powerful tool of today's education system.

Types of e-content

- **Assembled e-content:** it is the already published electronic resources collected and assembled from various sources.
- **Created e-content:** it is the e-content developed by the teacher or learner as his work.

Forms of E-content

- e-book
- e-journals
- videos
- audio clips
- digital text
- digital images
- graphics
- animation
- PowerPoint presentations
- simulative models
- quiz

Features/Advantages of E-content

- E-content is learner-friendly and learner-centric.
- It can be best used by teachers.
- E-content can include links to other resources.
- E-content uses multi-media such as text, audio, video, animation, etc.
- As it is stored in the cloud, it is permanent and will not be lost.
- E-content can be accessed anywhere and anytime.

E-content development

- E-content development is the process of designing and creating electronic content.
- Creation of e-content requires knowledge and skills in information technology and its application.
- E-content can be self-created or can be assembled from various sources.
- Systematic and scientific approach is needed for the development of e-content.
- The purpose of e-content development is to create an information-rich society.

Phases of e-content development

1. **Analysis phase:** it involves the analysis of the current situation and the determination of objectives, target audience, etc.
2. **Design phase:** it is the planning stage of e-content preparation.

3. **Development phase:** in this stage e-content is to be created by mixing text, audio, video, links, animation, etc.
4. **Testing phase:** prepared e-content is to be checked to ensure that it is free from spelling mistakes and other errors. It should be tested with the appropriate platform.
5. **Implementation phase:** e-content is to be made available to the targeted people through appropriate platforms.
6. **Evaluation phases:** collect feedback from learners and instructors to assess the effectiveness of e-content. It will be useful for the preparation of further materials.

E-content authoring tools

- It is a software package that developers use to create e-contents deliverables to end-users.
- It consists of all software used to create e-content such as MS PowerPoint, screen recorders, video editing software, PDF creators, learning management systems, etc.
- But the major tools that meet e-content learning standards include.

1. Sharable courseware object reference model(SCORM)
2. Aviation Industry CBT Committee(AICC)
3. Promoting multi-media access to education and training in European society (PROMETHEUS)
4. Advanced distributed learning initiatives(ADL)

Online libraries (digital libraries/virtual libraries)

- A digital library is a website that provides access to e-books, e-journals, and other collected learning resources.

- It is a collection of documents organized and stored in an electronic format that is accessible through the internet.
- Examples of digital libraries are the national digital library of India.

Features/advantages of digital libraries

- **Variety of digital content:** it offers digital content including books, articles, videos, audios, thesis, and other educational materials
- **No physical boundary:** no need to visit the library physically.
- Anytime availability: resources are available 24 hrs*7 days.
- **Multiple access:** same resources can be accessed by many users at the same time.
- **Searchability:** many search options are available to find appropriate resources.
- **Easy retrieval of information:** information can be retrieved easily in a suitable format with the least effort and minimum time.
- **Preservation and conservation:** books and other resources in digital form can be preserved for a long time. Unlike physical books, there is no chance of degradation due to repeated use.
- **Huge space:** huge local and cloud space is available to store resources.
- Added value: digitalization enhances clarity, legibility, etc.
- Low cost of maintenance: cost of maintenance is low compared to physical libraries.

Massive open online course (MOOC)

- The word MOOC was coined by Dave cornier in 2008.

- MOOC is an online course aimed at unlimited participation and open access through the internet.
- It is a web-based distance learning program.
- It is a model for delivering learning content online to any person who wants to take the course.
- It is free and students of any age can join the course.
- MOOCs are one of the most prominent trends in higher education in recent years.

MOOC

Massive- any number of students can join the course.

Open- anyone, anywhere can register for these courses free.

Online-course content is delivered entirely over the internet.

Course- structured around learning goals similar to another course

Features and advantages of MOOC

- Designed and implemented by educators
- a Large number of students can join
- All interested persons can participate
- No tuition fee.
- Open access
- Video lectures of top-level professors
- Video lectures are recorded and re-watchable
- Global sharing of knowledge
- It provides self-directed learning

Limitations of MOOC/Concerns about MOOC

- More chance of students dropping out
- Active feedback and discussion are not possible due to a large number of participants
- Students need to be self-motivated to learn
- E-literacy is an essential requirement
- Technical problems
- No formal degree awarded after the course
- Courses are available in limited languages, primarily in English
- Lack of certification or non-conventional certificates.

Emergent forms of MOOC types of courses

- **Open boundary course (OBC):** formally enrolled students and outsiders study together.
- **Small private online course (SPOC):** it is an online course designed for a specific small group of students. SPOCs often charge tuition fees.
- **Massive online course(MOC):** It is the online course available for anyone to enroll
- **Wrapped MOOC:** students in an on-campus course are asked to participate in a MOOC hosted by another institution.

MOOC platforms in India

1. **SWAYAM** (study webs of active learning for young aspiring minds)-meaning is "self".

- It is a MOOC launched by MHRD, the Government of India under the Digital India initiative.
- Courses delivered through SWAYAM are available free of cost, but learners who want a certificate have to pay an exam fee and

attend an online test at a designated center.

- To ensure the best quality content, nine institutions (AICTE, UGC, NCERT, IGNOU, etc.)are appointed as coordinators.
- SWAYAM Prabha is an education learning program initiated by MHRD through DTH channels.

2. **NPTEL**(national program on technology-enhanced learning):

- It is a project initiated by seven IITs and the Indian Institute of Science (IIS).
- It offers free online courses on engineering, science management, humanities, music, etc.

3. **Mookie:**

- It is an open-source MOOC management software developed by IIT Kanpur. They offer open online courses with mooKIT.

4. **IITBombayX:**

Other initiatives of the government of India toward e-learning &online education

- **Digital India**: it is the program launched to transform India into a digitally empowered society and knowledge economy.
- **Education and research network (ERNET):** Working for network connectivity in India.
- **EDUSAT:** satellite launched for education in India.
- **INFLIBNET** (information &library network): a platform for connecting all universities and colleges in India. It offers many services such as shodhganga, shodhgangotri, N-LIST, etc.
- **Consortium for educational communication (CEC):** an inter-university center set up by UGC to address the needs of higher

education through television

CHAPTER THREE

Business Analytics

Features of new generation computers:

• High speed of operation: computers can process millions of operations per second. Its speed is measured in terms of MHZ (megahertz) and GMZ(Gigahertz).
• Small and portable: modern computers are small in size and easily portable from one place to another.
• Accuracy: computers can perform a large number of tasks without errors.
• Huge storage: modern computers can store a huge volume of data.
• Reliability: it gives consistent results of a similar set of data.
• Versatility: computers can perform different types of work. Lots of tasks can be performed at the same time.
• Diligence: computers can work many hours continuously without taking any rest and without decreasing their speed, accuracy, and efficiency. It is free from fatigue and tiredness.
• Artificial intelligence: a computer can think and perform tasks like humans.
• Used for data analysis: computers are now widely used for data processing, storage, and analysis.
Data and information:
• Data is the raw facts that do not carry any specific meaning.

• Data is the unprocessed facts collected in their original form.
• When data is processed, it becomes information.
• Information is the organized and processed form of data that is meaningful.
• Eg: the age collected from 50 students in a class is data. But the table (prepared with the help of this data) which shows several students above and below the age of 18 is an example of information.
• Data analysis is the process of inspecting, cleaning, processing, and analyzing data to discover useful information.

Data analysis consists of the following stages (phases):

? Specification of data requirement: determination of the type of data needed.
? Data collection: a collection of primary and secondary data.
? Data cleaning: editing, removing errors, coding, etc.
? Data processing: conversion of data into useful information.
? Data analysis: analyzing data to draw interference and conclusion.
? Communication of results: reporting of the results.

Business data analysis (business analytics):

• Business analytics is the analysis of business data for decision-making.
• It is the process of collecting inspecting cleaning processing and modeling data to discover useful information in business.
• It uses statistical models and software packages.
• Business analytics helps managers to formulate policies take strategic decisions and solve complex problems.
Components of business analytics:
• Data warehousing: it consists of extraction of data from multiple

sources, cleaning, and storing in centralized databases called a data warehouse.

- Data mining (data processing): it is the process of discovering patterns and correlations in collected data. It includes text mining from social media sites.
- Data management: data governance and standards are required to ensure quality data.
- Data security: security analytics is used to ensure the privacy and security of data and to monitor malicious activity.
- Forecasting: forecast of future events and trends based on historical and current data. Predictive analysis is used for forecasting.
- Optimization: it is the use of simulation techniques to identify scenarios that will produce the best results.eg: sale prize optimization.
- Data visualization and reporting: interactive graphics and other visual images are used to present the output to management.

Types of business data analysis:

1. Descriptive analysis: (what is happening?)

- Descriptive analysis describes or summarizes the past and present data.
- It helps to understand what has happened in the past and what is happening currently.
- Descriptive statistics are used to analyze the data.
- Business intelligence is a subset of business analytics that focuses on descriptive analysis.
- Eg: monthly sales reports of a company.

2. Diagnostic analysis (why it is happening?)

- Diagnostic analysis helps to find out the reasons for happening things (positive and negative) revealed in descriptive analysis.

• It examines the past performance to determine what happened and why.

• It helps to find out the reasons behind problems and issues in business and troubleshoot them.

• Eg: sales analysis to find out the causes of low sales volume in the past quarter.

3. Predictive analysis (what is likely to happen):

• This analysis helps to predict and forecast future events and trends with the help of past data.

• It uses data mining statistical models machine learning Automation artificial intelligence etc. to extract trends from existing data and form predictions.

• Predictive analytics allows organizations to become proactive and forward-looking.

• Eg: estimation of future sales (sales budget) to plan production.

4. Prescriptive analysis (what do I need to do?):

• Prescriptive analytics make use of the information received from all other analysis and forms a plan of action for the business organization.

• It helps to choose the desired course of action among the available alternatives to achieve the objectives and goals of the business.

• It also prescribes steps to avoid future problems and loss.

• Number of tools with built-in prescriptive analytics is now available to provide users the actionable results.

• Eg: a plan of action for the launching of a new product.

Tools of business analytics:

• Business analytics tools are software solutions that can be used to analyze business data.

• These are application software that can be used for descriptive diagnostic predictive and prescriptive analysis.

• Number of proprietaries and open source software is now available for the use of business analytics.
• Most organizations use more than one analytical tool.
Examples of popular business analytics tools:
• Open source tools/software
R: used by Google, Facebook, etc.
PYTHON: used by Alibaba, Google, etc.
APACHE SPARK: used by Ola, Uber, Infosys, etc.
PIG&HIVE: used by Facebook, yahoo, Flip kart, etc.
• Proprietary tools/software
SAS: used by Google, Citibank, HDFC, etc.
TABLEAU: used by Toyota, dell, hp, Ashok Leyland, etc.
MICROSOFT EXCEL: Used by almost every company.
SPLUNK: used by adobe, coca-cola, etc.
Emerging trends in business analytics:
• Business intelligence: it is a sub-set of business analytics that mostly focuses on descriptive analysis(not prescriptive)
• Big data analysis: it is the process of examining a large amount of complex data to discover hidden patterns market trends correlations customer preferences etc.
• Artificial intelligence: all-enabled business analytics tools help the business to manage business data better.
• Security analytics: it is a combination of software algorithms and analytic processes used to detect potential threats to IT systems.
• Data quality analytics: it is always working for the improvement of the quality of business data generated and collected.
• Internet of things: the data generated through devices with internet connectivity can be used to control the data management process.
• Cloud analytics: it is the use of cloud private and public computing resources available on the internet to analyze data.it is available either on a subscription or pays for work basis.
• Social networking analytics: it is the process of gathering and analyzing data from social media networks such as Facebook, Instagram, Twitter, etc. for the use of business decisions.

• Augmented analytics: it is the use of machine learning artificial intelligence, natural language processing, etc. to enhance data analytics data sharing, and business intelligence.

Importance/advantages of business analytics:

• Ensure data quality: it ensures the collected data is relevant and appropriate.

• Provides updated data: business analytics always provide updated data for managerial decision-making.

• Assist in business decision making: business analytics provides the right information to facilitate strategic decisions in business.

• Helps to foresee future challenges: predictive and prescriptive analysis helps to predict future events and thereby the business can overcome the future challenges.

• Improves operational efficiency of business: decision making with the help of business analytics reduces the costs and improves the efficiency of functional areas such as product marketing etc.

• Competitive advantages: business firms utilizing business analytics will be better than that competitor who does not.

• Improved customer service: the analysis of customer data helps to provide better services to the customers.

• Evaluation of progress: it helps to evaluate how much of the mission and objective of the business is accomplished.

Disadvantages/challenges of business analytics:

• Cost and complexity: it is a complex system and a lot of human financial and technical resources are required to implement it. The employee must have technical skills to utilize the system.

• Data security: implementation of a proper security system is the main challenge. If data is not secured the company may face cyber attacks and other data loss issues.

• Lack of commitment: since the business users do not see the promised results immediately, they may lose interest which results in a loss of trust.

• Danger of low-quality data: if the quality of data used for business analytics is poor, it gives negative results.

Business Data Analyst

• Business data analyst is a person responsible for data analysis in business.
• Data analysts collect, process, and analyses data to make available the required information for business decisions.
• Data analyst discovers how data can be used to answer questions and solve problems in business.
• He must possess the required knowledge and skill to work as a business data analyst.
• A degree in analytics or a related field is a desirable qualification.

Knowledge & Skills Required For Data Analyst

• Knowledge in data warehousing: knowledge in data extraction, data cleansing, and loading data to a centralized location called a data warehouse.
• Data mining skills: skills to process and analyze data to draw meaningful patterns.
• Knowledge about analytical tools – such as R, Python, SAS, Microsoft Excel, etc.
• Statistical skills: proficiency in mathematics and statistics.
• Reporting skills: he must know the way and format of business reporting.
• Data visualization: A good analyst must know what types of visualization techniques such as charts, graphs, animation, etc., is to be used for reporting.
• Machine learning; It is a fundamental skill such as computer architecture, algorithms, programming languages, etc.
• Communication skills: He must have strong and effective interpersonal skills such as communication skills to convey the findings of the analysis.
• Other hard skills and soft skills – He must have other soft skills and hard skills to perform his duties.

Duties & Responsibilities of a Data Analyst

- Design and maintenance: designing and maintaining data systems and databases, including troubleshooting potential issues.
- Data warehousing: it is the process of extracting data from multiple sources, and cleaning and storing data in centralized databases.
- Data mining: analysis of large data to discover meaningful patterns and useful information from it.
- Data interpretation: interpretation of data with the help of statistical techniques.
- Forecasting: forecast future events based on past and current data to avoid future contingencies in business.
- Preparing reports: prepare reports which effectively communicate their findings to organizational leadership and key stakeholders.
- Making recommendations; preparing strategic recommendations for process adjustments, procedures, and performance improvements.
- Collaborate with others: as an employee of the business, he has to work in collaboration with other departments and key persons such as programmers, engineers, etc.

Types of Analysts in Business

1. Data Analyst

- Data analysts gather data, manipulate it, identify useful information from it, and transform their findings into trends and insights
- Analyzing data to uncover trends and insights is their main goal.
- They must have knowledge and skills in tools of data analysis.

2. Business Analyst

- Business analysts evaluate business processes and use data to make strategic business decisions and find solutions to business problems.

• Business decision-making and the implementation of changes based on decisions are their end goals.

• Business analysts must have industry experience.

3. System Analyst (Business Technology Analyst)

• Systems analysts study an organization's current computer systems and procedures.

• System analysts design information system solutions to help the organization operate more efficiently and effectively.

• They design computer-based systems for various types of business data analysis and train others to use the system.

4. Process Analyst (Operation Research Analyst)

• Process analysts examine business processes and recommend ways to improve and automate these processes. They analyze data to ensure the operational efficiency of the business. They help businesses to make their business processes cost-effective and efficient.

5. User Experience Analyst (Ux Analyst)

• They are professionals involved in the design of the user interface of software and websites according to user requirements.

• User interface is the front and view of the application software which allows the user to interact with it.

• They analyze user experiences to improve the interface further.

6. Change Analyst (Change Management Analyst)

• They are analysts responsible for implementing new methods and changes in the business.

• Change analysts analyze data to recommend new systems and

organizational changes to improve organizational efficiency.
• They also help management to implement and monitor changes.

7. Data Engineer

• Data engineers are focused on building infrastructure and architecture for data generation analysis.
• They are software engineers who design and build infrastructure for big data analysis.
• They are responsible for the development and maintenance of software and tools for the use of other analysts.

8. Data Scientist

• Data scientist is an expert data analyst.
• Data scientists are analytical experts who utilize their skills in both technology and social science to find trends and manage data to solve complex problems in business.
• They are experts in big data analysis.
• They make use of the latest technologies in analyzing data and finding solutions to business problems.
• They possess knowledge of mathematics, statistics, computer science, machine learning algorithms, programming, etc.
• Many data scientists began their careers as data analysts.

Role and responsibilities of Data Scientists in Business:

? Empower management to make sound decisions.
? Search for new data sources and assess their accuracy.
? Familiarize employees using the analytics systems.
? Recommend actions to improve performance.
? Create data models and algorithms.

? Big data analysis.
? Identify ways for improving the current analytics system.
? Use predictive models to forecast future events, future challenges, etc.
? Test and evaluate the outcome of managerial decisions.
? Coordinates with various technical/functional teams to implement models and monitor results.
? Recruitment of talented employees.

Role of data science and data scientists in society:

- They are enablers of next-generation innovations.
- Helps to identify the requirements of the society.
- Provide customers with the best value based on prediction data.
- Governments are now utilizing data science in social planning and implementation of social policies.
- Data science is also used widely in the health sector, media, etc.
- They provide solutions for societal challenges.

Artificial intelligence:

- Artificial intelligence is the ability of a machine or computer to perform those tasks which need human intelligence. It is the intelligence artificially created for machines.
- It is not a replacement for human intelligence but serves as a supporting tool. All make it possible for computers to learn from experience adjust to new situations and perform human-like tasks.

Intelligent agent in AI:

- An intelligent agent is a computer program or robot capable to act intelligently on behalf of a user. An intelligent agent is a robot or program with artificial intelligence that can make decisions or perform a service based on experiences, user inputs, and available information.

Artificial intelligence and intelligent agents in business:

• Artificial intelligence is now widely used in business to make the job smarter and faster.

• Artificial intelligence is mainly used for the following purpose in business

i. Automating business processes.

ii. Gaining insight through data analysis and engaging with customers and employees.

iii. It is one of the most important tools used in electronic commerce.

Role of artificial intelligence and intelligence agents in e-business:

• Sales forecasting: it is used in analyzing a huge volume of user data and to make sales forecasts on basis of these data.

• Chatbots: they are robots or software capable to conduct text or voice chat over a network. Chatbots are now widely used in business for providing 24hrs *7 days of customer support.

• Customer relationship management: AI is used to store and analyze customer data and helps businesses to maintain successful relationships with them to repeat sales.

• Personalized content:

1. AI is used by e-commerce sites to collect and analyze customer interest and shopping behavior

2. These data are used to show content suitable to the customer and to make product recommendations based on previous searches and purchase

• **Product comparisons**: artificial intelligence is also employed by commerce sites to show product comparisons relevant to the search history of the user.

- **Inventory management**: AI is used to manage the right level of inventory and to avoid the idle stock.
- **Marketing solutions**: AI is used in marketing for a wide variety of purposes. it is used for sending marketing emails, supply chain automation personalized advertisements, etc.
- **Customer satisfaction**: AI is employed to collect the exact needs and wants of the consumers and thereby helps the vendor to ensure customer satisfaction.
- **shopping experience:** it is used to create customer-centric search facilities and a variety of shopping experiences in the commerce website and app.

Ethical and legal considerations in business analytics:

- Business organizations that make use of data analytics must address the ethical use of data.
- There should be a common code of ethics and standards to be followed by analytic professionals similar to other industries.
- These standards should be formulated by the relevant cyber acts or IT regulations of the country and the world.
- There are a lot of such ethical and legal considerations that need to be recognized in connection with business analytics.

Ethical and legal considerations in business analytics:

- Does not violate copyright regulations: while using copyrighted data the firm has to ensure that the copyright regulations are not violated.
- **Comply with legal requirements:** the process of business analytics must be designed in such a way as to comply with all laws and regulations such as the IT act.
- **Ethical code of conduct:** an ethical code of conduct is to be framed for the organization and the same shall be communicated to

all members.

• **Ensure data privacy:** privacy of consumer data is to be ensured and proper precautions should be taken to avoid the abuse of private data. Private data obtained from a person with their consent cannot be shared with others.

• **Ensure data security:** the company should implement appropriate measures to ensure the security of data used for analytics.

• **Ensure accountability**: hold business professionals and analysts accountable for all actions. They must realize the power of the data they are handling and the damage that it can do if it is received in the wrong hands.

• **Cultural and social norms**: the company should ensure that the business analytics is not violating the social and cultural norms.

Social networking analysis:

• Social is the social relationship among individuals, families, households, communities, etc.

• Internet-based social media such as Facebook, what's app etc. now plays a vital role in creating social networks.

• Social networking analysis is the practice of gathering data from social media and analyzing that data to make business decisions.

Social network analysis and business analytics:

• Social network analysis is an integral part of business analytics. Social network analysis is one of the main sources of data for business analytics.

• Social network analysis helps businesses in discovering the patterns of interactions between people.

• This data is utilized for determining customer behavior understanding market trends solving human resources problems etc.

Steps in social network analysis:

- Identify social networks.
- Collect social interaction data from the networks.
- Analysis of data with the help of s/w and tools such as sociogram.
- Reporting-presentation of results to the users.

Business and other applications of social network analysis (uses and benefits):

- Analysis of consumer behavior: social network analysis can be used to collect customer data such as customer profile customer behavior customer preferences customer needs buying motives etc.
- Solving human resource problems: social network analysis can be conducted to identify the problems of employees and to find solutions.
- Enable organizational change: it is useful to identify the formal and the informal social network within the organization. Analysis of group relationships within these networks can be used to improve business performance.
- Understanding health behavior: people communicate health data through social networks. It is useful for hospitals, government, etc. for designing health plans.
- Identification of criminal and terrorist networks: through analyzing the communication between social networks, government and law enforcement agencies can identify criminal and terrorist networks.
- Improvement of communication flow: SNA helps to analyze and improve communication flow in every organization.
- Useful for network operators: network and mobile operators can use SNA to optimize the structure and capacity of their networks.

Big data:

• Big data refers to the large volume of data both structured and unstructured. It is in the form of text, video, audio, images, etc.
• Big data refers to complex and large data sets that have to be processed and analyzed to uncover valuable information that can benefit businesses organization.
• Now we are in the 'age of big data which is produced by computers and other forms of technology.
• Businesses, government health care providers financial institutions academic institutions, etc. are now utilizing the power of big data.

Big data analysis:

• Big data analysis is the process of analyzing big data.
• It is the process of examining a large amount of data to uncover information such as hidden patterns, correlations, market trends, customer preferences, etc., for managerial decisions.
• Big data cannot be processed or analyzed using conventional data processing techniques.
• Big data analytics uses advanced analytic techniques for the analysis of big data.
• Extract, transform and load (ETL) is the process of preparing data for analysis.

Types of big data:

Structured data:

- It is the data in an organized form.
- It is the data that can be processed and stored in a fixed format.
- Eg: employee information in a company database(textual data)

Unstructured data:

- It is the data that lacks a specific form.
- It is very difficult to process and analyze unstructured data.
- Eg: contents of email which consist of text, images, videos, etc.

Semi-structured data:

- It is the combination of structured and unstructured data.
- It is partly structured data.

Four dimensions of big data (4 'v's):

- **Volume:** volume refers to the quantity of data. Volume may be measured in terms of bytes. KB, MB, GB, TB, PB, EB, ZB, YB.
- **Variety:** refers to a diversified type of data and source of data.it consists of structured, semi-structured, and unstructured data.
- **Veracity**: refers to the biases, errors, and abnormalities in data. Big data analysis employs cleaning and processing of data to avoid veracity.
- **Velocity**: it refers to the speed with which data is generated from various sources. The real-time data helps business firms for taking timely decisions.

Technologies for gathering and processing big data:

- Business intelligence.
- Data warehousing.
- Data mining.

- Data modeling.
- Cloud computing.
- Statistical tools.
- Software solutions.

Steps in big data analysis (components):

- **Data extraction and integration:** a collection of data from multiple sources.
- **Data cleaning and organization:** remove errors and transform the data into an analyzable form.
- **Storage:** loading of data and processed information in offline and online databases.
- **Analysis:** analysis of data with the help of statistical and software tools.
- **Consumption**: presenting the information in the right format to the end-user.

Advantages of big data:

- Improved business processes and productivity: big data helps to improve the operational efficiency of the firm continuously with minimum cost and effort.
- Greater innovation: big data analysis helps the business to introduce new technologies and products.
- Cost reduction: the initial cost of big data analysis is high, but it is useful to reduce the cost in the long run.
- Support decision-making: big data analysis provides relevant and updated information for decision-making at various management levels.
- Competitive advantage: if a company gets early data relating to its

rivals and their strategies the policies and strategies of the company can be well formulated to get a competitive advantage.

• Improved customer service: big data helps to understand the customer needs and wants and thereby serve the customers better.

• Early detection of errors and frauds: big data analysis helps to mitigate losses by quickly detecting the errors and frauds.

• Profitability and growth of the business: operational efficiency smart decisions better marketing strategies improved customer services etc.

Limitations:

• High cost of implementation: the implementation of a big data analysis system in the organization is costly and complex.

• Needs technical expertise: a lot of staff with technical expertise is needed to collect and analyze big data.

• Storage: the firm has to spend a lot of money to store data securely.

• Mostly unstructured: the majority of big data is unstructured which needs cleaning organization and processing.

• Data quality issues: more information also means more false and useless information. The use of low-quality data may yield a negative result.

• Privacy and security: it is very difficult to ensure the privacy and security of data used in big data analysis. Data should be kept free from cyber-attacks.

• Social stratification: the use of big data by businesses and government may lead to the categorization of people based on socio-economic factors like income education etc.

• No short-run benefits: big data analysis is not useful in the short run.

It is to be employed in the long run to get the benefit.

Data Quality Management

Data, Information & Knowledge:
• Data is the raw facts that do not carry any specific meaning
• Information is the organized and processed form of data that is meaningful.
• The understanding and applicability of the information in a particular situation (for taking decisions) are called knowledge.
• Data, information, and knowledge are the inputs of business analytics that are used for taking managerial decisions.

Organization of Data:

• Organization of data refers to the systematic arrangements of data for processing and analysis.
• The user can quickly gather the required information only if the data is organized properly.
• It consists of data cleaning, classification, and storage at appropriate places.
Importance of Data Organization:
• It decreases the time consuming to search for data.
• Organizing data helps in reducing data loss.
• Data organization helps to reduce data errors.
• It helps to understand why the data was collected and how to use it effectively.
• It makes analysis and interpretation easy.
• It facilitates the comparison of data.
• It helps to simplify complex data.

Sources / Methods of Collecting Primary Data:

- **Observation:** watching people and objects and perceiving data through senses. Data relating to the customers, employees, stock, market conditions, etc., can be collected through observation.
- **Interview:** the interview is a purposeful discussion where questions are asked by the interviewer to elicit information. Interviews may be conducted with customers, employees, market intermediaries, etc., to collect data.
- **Survey:** it is the collection of data by using questionnaires. Census or sample surveys may be conducted among customers, employees, dealers, suppliers, etc.
- **Experimentation:** experimentation involves the manipulation of one variable to determine its effect on other variables. Example: assessment of the impact of advertising on sales.
- **Warranty cards**: in this method, postal size cards (warranty cards) are used by dealers of consumer durables to collect information regarding their products.
- **Distribution audit**: in this method, salesmen are sent by dealers to retail stores at regular intervals to collect data at sales points.
- **Pantry audit:** in this method, data is recorded by observing or examining the consumer's pantry (shopping basket).

Data Quality:

- Data quality is the ability of data to serve an intended purpose.
- Data quality is measured in terms of its accuracy, completeness, consistency, reliability, and updating.
- In business, data quality is the capability of data to satisfy the requirements of a business enterprise.
- Business data is said to be high quality if it is best suited for taking managerial decisions.

Data Integrity vs. Data Quality

• Data integrity is a broader concept that combines data quality, data governance, and data protection mechanisms.
• Data integrity is the accuracy, completeness, reliability, and security of data throughout its lifecycle.
Components / Parameters of Data Quality
• **Accuracy:** data should be correct and free from errors.
• **Completeness:** it should include all material facts. There will be no missing aspects in the data.
• **Reliability (consistency):** if a particular data item is taken from multiple data sets, it should be the same in content and format. Data must be collected by using the measurement scale which produces consistent results.
• **Relevance:** the data must be suitable to the given purpose for which it is collected.
• **Validity:** if the collected data is exactly what is intended, it is said to be valid. It must be in the right format, collected through the right process, and falls within the right range.
• **Timeliness:** it is to be collected at the right time and made available at the time of managerial decisions.
• Updating: data should be new, recently collected, or updated regularly.

Data Quality Management (DQM):

• It is the process of ensuring data quality in business at all times.
• It is the practice of a system that consistently tries to improve the quality of data.
• It is the process of ensuring the accuracy, reliability, relevance, completeness, and security of data.

Importance of Data Quality in Business:

• **Avoid errors**: it avoids operational errors and business process breakdowns.
• **Better business decisions**: it enables timely decisions in all functional areas such as production, HRM, marketing, finance, etc.
• **Competitive advantage**: useful to gain a competitive advantage over other firms in the industry.
• **Make business analytics efficient**: data quality determines the success of business analytics.
• **Better customer targeting**: assessment of exact customer requirements helps to design marketing mix elements such as product, price, promotion, and distribution.
• **Improved customer relationship:** accurate customer data helps to maintain a good relationship with the customers.
• **Growth and profitability of business**: A business that makes use of quality data will grow in terms of market share and profitability.

How to Ensure Data Quality?

• **Well-structured data collection plan:** the data requirement and data collection process are to be planned well.
• **Build & train a data quality team:** appoint and train suitable persons to manage the process of data collection, processing, and analysis.
• **Efficient business analytics system**: an efficient business analytics system is to be established in the organization to manage data.
• Use data quality tools – such as;
• **Data quality standards**: type of data needed, data format, its representation, etc. are to be prescribed well in advance.
• **Data cleaning**: it is the process of removing incorrect and duplicate data.
• Ensure timely distribution of data: ensure timely distribution of

data across departments for taking decisions.

Missing / Incomplete Data

• One of the most common problems in data analytics is the management of missing data.
• Missing data is the data element that is required but omitted.
• Example: a question in the questionnaire which is not answered by many respondents.

Types of Missing Data:

• **Structurally missing data:** data is missing because it does not exist. For example, the ages of children are missing because these people have no children.
• **Missing Completely At Random (MCAR):** some data is missed, but there is no systematic difference between observed data and missed data. So the analysis remains unbiased due to the absence of missed data. (example: when we take a random sample, some are selected and some are omitted)
• **Missing At Random (MAR):** some data is missed, and there is a systematic difference between the observed data and missed data. The analysis may be biased due to the absence of missed data. (example: a randomly selected respondent fails to provide correct information because of ill-health)\
• **Missing Not At Random (MNAR):** data is neither MCAR nor MAR. Data is missing because of the reasons unknown to us.

Dealing With Missing Data (Techniques of Handling Missing Data)

- **Listwise deletion/case deletion:** remove all data of an observation that has one missing value. It leads to a reduction in the total sample size. (example: remove a questionnaire with one missing answer)
- Pairwise deletion: the variable with missing data is only deleted from a specific observation. It is generally done when the influence of one variable on another is analyzed. (example: in correlation analysis, remove the missing value of a particular question of that sample only)
- **Mean substitution:** The mean value of the other variables is taken in place of missing data. For example: if the age of one respondent is missed, the average age of other respondents is taken as the age of missing respondents.
- **Regression imputation:** it is the process of replacing the missing value with the value estimated with the help of regression analysis. Regression analysis helps to predict unknown values with the help of known values.
- **Last observation carried forward:** missing value is replaced with last observed value.
- **Maximum likelihood:** missing data is estimated by using the parameters (mean, standard deviation, etc.) calculated with the help of available data.
- **Multiple imputations:** missing data is replaced by a set of possible values one after another and analyzed separately. By combining these analysis results, a single overall result is produced. Sensitivity is used to specify sets of observations.

CHAPTER FOUR

Socio - Cyber Informatics

Social Informatics

- Social Informatics is an emerging area of informatics that studies the social aspects of information and Communication Technologies (ICT)
- It is the study of information and communication tools in social or institutional contexts.
- It examines the role of IT in the development of organizations and society.
- It examines the opportunities and threats created by ICT in business and society.

IT and Society

- Now we are living in the age of information technology
- The widespread availability of computers and the internet provides us with a lot of opportunities to learn and communicate.
- Technology has had many positive effects on society but has also impacted society in many negative ways.

- Some individuals exploit the power of information technology for criminal, terrorist, and other undesirable purposes. It has created many unresolved ethical and social issues in the society

Positive impacts of IT on Society

- Faster communication with lower cost
- Paperless environment
- Automation of dangerous tasks
- Technology innovations.
- Better management of data(collection, storage, processing & retrieval)
- Applications in business, education, healthcare, banking, research, administration, entertainment, etc.
- Cost reduction, time-saving, etc.

Social and Ethical Issues of Information Technology

- Privacy and Freedom
- IPR (Privacy and Copyright issues)
- System quality
- Automation and employment
- Conflict between Digital natives and digital immigrants
- Digital divide
- Health issues
- Social implications of E-Governance
- Other Cyberspace issues (Cyber addiction, Cybercrime, Cyber abuse, Cyber waste, Information overload, Green computing, etc.)

1.

Privacy and freedom:

- Privacy is the right of an individual to be left alone.
- The information that we provide to the govt and agencies is stored in computers and other databases of these agencies. This information may be misused and thereby affect the privacy of individuals.
- Information sent over the internet may pass through many computer systems before it reaches the recipient. Some people or websites collect and store this information without the consent of the user.
- Special software like cookies is used to trace the details of the visitors.
- To protect the right to privacy almost all countries of the world have enacted laws but unimplemented practically.

1.

IPR (Privacy and Copyright issues)

- Right given to people for the reproduction of something which are the creations of their mind or intellect is called Intellectual Property Rights. (Example: Patent, copyright, etc.)
- Information Technology raises a great challenge to the existing IPRs.
- It is easy to copy, alter and spread books and materials over the internet (Copying the work of others and using it as own work is called Plagiarism)
- Many people upload copyrighted music, videos, and cinemas.
- Software piracy is another issue related to the violation of IPR. (Software piracy refers to the unauthorized duplication of computer software)

- Software piracy is widespread from individual computer users to professionals and government institutions.
- It is estimated that more than 35% of the software installed in the world is unlicensed or cracked.
- The present laws are not adequate to restrict piracy, plagiarism, and other copyright issues.

3.

System quality

- Many organizations and Government agencies are making use of many software for various purposes.
- System failure, corruption of software, loss of data, connectivity issues, etc., creates problems in service sectors including the government services.
- Uninterrupted power supply, paper alternatives, proper backup, and security elements should be implemented to overcome the issues.

4.

Automation and Employment:

- Introduction of computers in many business and social applications reduced some types of job opportunities.
- Many routines and monotonous jobs formerly done by clerks are now replaced by computers.
- However, if a computer is introduced in a particular area, several new job opportunities requiring new skills and education are created.
- Computerisation reduces the employment opportunities of unskilled jobs only.
- Computerisation reduces the employment opportunities of unskilled jobs only.

- The computer and communication industry itself has created many job opportunities in hardware and software.

5.

Conflicts between Digital Natives and Digital Immigrants

- Digital natives are the new generation of young people born into the digital age.
- Digital natives are tech-savvy people interacting with technology from childhood.
- Digital immigrants are those who learned to use computers at some stage during their adult life.
- Majority of the digital immigrants struggle to adopt the technology.
- The gap between digital natives and digital immigrants creates conflicts in the family, education, workplace, etc.

6.

Digital Divide

- Digital Divide is the gap between people who have access to digital technology and those who have no or little access.
- It is the gap between digital literates and illiterates.
- Digital divide may have implications in various sectors and services of the economy.
- Digital divide keeps people in certain social groups based on their computer knowledge.

7.

Health Problems:

- Extensive and excessive use of computers and the internet will create many health problems, both physical and mental.
- Example:
    - Physical: Stress in eyes, Finger pain, back pain, headaches,
    - Mental: Impatience, fatigue, depression, low family relationship, etc.

8.

Social Implications of E-Governance

- E-Governance is the application of Information technology in delivering Government services to society.
- Number of Government services are now provided through electronic media such as the internet.
- Digital illiteracy, Digital divide, low connectivity, poor IT infrastructure, high cost of IT, etc., creates problems for the society in accessing e-services of Government.

9.

Other Cyberspace issues

- **Cyber addiction**- It is the excessive use of computers and the internet.
- **Cyber Crime**: It is the crime that either targets a computer or is committed through a computer network.
- **Cyber abuse**: It is the use of technology to hurt someone socially or psychologically.
- **Cyber waste**: It is the waste created by discarded electronic and electrical devices.
- **Information overload**: It refers to the difficulty in understanding due to the availability of excess data.

- **Green Computing:** It is the environmentally responsible and eco-friendly use of computers, the internet, and other technologies.

Digital Divide

- Digital divide refers to the gap between people who possess regular access to information technology and those who do not have this access.
- It is the gap between people who use computers and the internet and those who do not.
- It is the inequalities among the people in the access to digital technologies.
- Due to the increased use of computers and the internet, the digital divide may be smaller in developed countries. However, the situation will be different in an underdeveloped or developing country.
- Some the education institutions can adapt technology whereas some poorly funded schools and colleges may not be able to offer technology to their students.
- So some people in the society get an advantage over those who are technically poor.
- It creates problems in accessing e-governance services, innovative financial services, etc.
- Digital divide keeps people in certain social groups based on their computer knowledge.

Aspects of Digital Divide

Access (Access divide):

- It is the gap between the people with access and those without access to ICT.

Usage (Use divide):

- It is the gap between people who know how to use technology and those who do not.

Usage Quality (Quality of use gap):

- It is the gap between people who are experts in ICT and others who are ordinary users.

Reasons for (Factors Contributing to) Digital Divide

- **Gender:**Females have less access to IT in certain countries, religions, and races. It affects the principle of gender equality
- **Income:** The income gap plays a considerable role in magnifying the digital divide. High-income earners are more likely to access IT and the internet than low-income earners.
- **Availability of infrastructure:**Some countries and areas are blessed with sufficient infrastructure to access IT while the infrastructure is poor in some other areas.
- **Cost of access:** High cost of electronic devices, high cost of internet, etc., creates a digital divide among low-income groups and rural people.
- **Education:** Illiteracy and Low Education levels are widening the digital inequality gap. Educated people may have more access to the full potential of the internet and computers.
- **Geographic location:** People living in urban areas have access to a wide variety of technology and high-speed internet compared to rural people.

- **Computer illiteracy:** Students who got a computer education have an advantage over those who do not.
- **Age:** Young people (Digital natives) feel more comfortable using IT and the internet compared to older people (Digital immigrants)
- **Cultural & behavioral attitudes:** Many people thought that IT and the internet are harmful and therefore not essential.
- **Family structure:** People from different family backgrounds are different in IT access and usage. Families with children may have more IT access than families without children.

Impact/Effects of Digital Divide on Society

- **Economic Inequalities among people:** Those who have access to modern technology can engage in more economically productive activities. These people can achieve more economic progress compared to others.
- **Impact on Education:** Students who have access to computers and the internet can acquire valuable information from the internet for their education & research. Lack of IT access will be a barrier to studies and research.
- **Impact on the economy:** Economic growth of a country depends on the digital divide. The high digital divide minimizes productivity and economic growth.
- **Impact on the society:** It may create many issues in the society such as gender discrimination, stratification of society, etc. The use of the internet can lead to a better democratic setup.
- **Impact on Culture:** Technology creates both positive and negative impacts on culture. The developed countries experience tremendous changes in their culture because of the adaption of technology. But the culture of developing countries is unchanged because they do not have access to technology.

- **Problems in accessing e-services:** It creates problems in accessing e-services such as electronic banking, e-commerce, e-governance, etc.

Measures to overcome Digital Divide

- **Compulsory computer education:** Free and compulsory education must be provided for lower primary **classes.**
- **Digital literacy programs:**Digital literacy programs should be initiated on the part of the Government, banks, social agencies, educational institutions, etc., to the adult people. Make people understand the benefit of using technology and how to use technology.
- **Affordable internet to all:**High-speed internet facility is to be provided in all areas. Free internet must be provided to socially and economically backwardpeople.
- **Provide access to technology:** Electronics devices must be made available to the people at a reasonable cost. Special schemes to buy a laptop and smartphones must be initiated for students.
- Help people with special needs: Special care should be given to the physically or mentally disabled people, people with lower social classes, etc., for meeting their IT needs.
- **Digital libraries in educational institutions:** Digital libraries with computers and the internet must be ensured in all educational institutions.
- **Sufficient number of E-services centers:** Sufficient number of e-services centers such as Akshaya must be ensured in all areas. Special concessions in services charges must be offered to the socially and economically backward people.

Digital Natives

- The term Digital Native is coined by Mark Prensky in 2001.
- Digital natives are the new generation of young people born into the digital age.
- Digital natives are tech-savvy people interacting with technology from childhood.
- They are very comfortable with using technology and understand that technology is essential for the success of life.

Types of Digital Natives

- **Gen Y (Generation Y)** - People who were born between 1980-1995 are considered first-generation digital natives.
- **Gen Z (Generation Z)** - People born after 1995.
- **Avoiders:** They were born in the digital age but are not interested in digital technology. For example, Digital natives who have smartphones but do not use email and social networking apps.
- **Minimalists:** They were born in the digital age but the technology is used only for limited essential purposes.
- **Enthusiastic participants:** They are digital natives who enjoy using digital technology. They are the regular users of smartphones, laptops, email, social media, e-commerce, electronic banking, etc.

Digital Natives Vs Digital Immigrants
Digital Natives Digital Immigrants

- People who were born after 1980
- Categorised as Gen Y (Born 1980-95) & (Born after 1995)
- Children & young people
- Born into the digital age
- Learnt to use a computer, smartphone, and internet in childhood
- Majority are tech-savvy.

- Majority enjoy using technology
- People who were born before 1980
- Categorised as Baby boomers (1945-65) & Gen X (1965-1980)
- Middle-aged and old aged people
- Born before the digital age
- Learnt to use technology in their adult life only.
- Majority is Luddite.
- Majority struggle to use technology

Business Strategies for Digital Natives

- Establish the brand & values.
- Use digital marketing – Content marketing, email marketing, social media marketing, mobile marketing, etc.
- Try to build good online reviews.
- Establish both offline and online trading
- Provide all e-payment options
- Use the latest and updated technology
- Highlight dedication to privacy.
- Practice customer relationship marketing
- Ensure good after-sale support etc.

What is CyberSpace?

- Cyberspace is the virtual world created by computers and the internet.
- It is the global computer network that facilities online communication.
- It is the virtual space for information and communication.
- It permits the processing, manipulation, exploration, and augmentation of information.

- It also facilitates interaction and communication between people living all over the globe.

Cyber Space: Opportunities

- **Information resources:** It is a virtual library of searchable information available 24*7 days. It can be utilized better in business analytics, education, research, etc.
- **Communication:** It enables us to interact and communicate with people all over the globe. Wireless communications such as Bluetooth and Wi-Fi provide a lot of opportunities in education, business, and other fields.
- **Social Networking:** It is a great medium to connect with millions of people with similar interests. Social media can be best utilized for marketing the products and services of a business.
- **Business space:** It is the space that can be utilized for business firms for data analytics, marketing, etc.
- **Electronic banking:** Cyberspace facilities fast and secure online payments such as online banking, mobile payments, wallets, open banking (UPI), etc.
- **E-commerce:** The growth and development of e-commerce provide opportunities for both large and small firms.
- **Outsourcing:** The development of cyberspace pave the way for IT infrastructure outsourcing, Business process outsourcing, etc.
- **Internet of Things:** Smart devices and machines with internet connectivity are widely used in business, education, etc.
- **Artificial intelligence:** Artificial intelligence can solve complex problems efficiently in multiple industries such as education, healthcare, finance, cyber security, astronomy, etc.

- **Cloud computing:** Cloud computing facilitates secure storage and access of apps, data, and internet-based services from any location worldwide.
- **IT Industry opportunities-** Development in IT provides a lot of business and job opportunities in Hardware, software services, cyber security, IT consulting, Network integration, etc.
- **Other:** Cyberspace has opened up opportunities in the entertainment industry, e-Governance, healthcare, travel, tourism, education, etc

Cyberspace: Issues and Threats

1. **Privacy & security of data**

- Data privacy is the right of individuals to have control over their personal information.
- The data share in cyberspace may be collected and misused by others. It hurt the basic human right of privacy.
- The privacy and security threats generated by the internet are increasing day by day.
- There is no comprehensive legal framework that deals with the privacy issue.

2. **Malware**

- Malware refers to malicious software.
- Malware is any software intentionally designed to cause damage to a computer, program, data, or network.
- It may infect computer programs, delete files, duplicate data, steals data, affect hardware, etc.
- There are a lot of malware types and some common malware are;
- Computer Virus

- Trojan Horses
- Adware
- Computer Worms
- Spyware
- Ransomware etc.

Virus (Vital Information Under Siege)

- Computer Virus is a malicious program that can spread from one computer to another.
- It is generally attached to an executable program or file and will infect the computer when the user runs or open it. A virus lays dormant in the system until the user executive it.
- Some viruses are harmless and some others can damage the files, software, or hardware.

Computer Worms

- It is a malicious program that replicates itself and spread quickly across computer networks.
- Unless viruses, worms are self-sufficient programs that do not require a host program or file.
- It will be executed independently and spread over a computer network.
- Similar to viruses, worms are capable to infect data, cause network failure, destroy files, etc.

Trojan Horse

- It is malicious software that can take control of a computer and create a backdoor entry for hackers and malicious programs.
- It is used by hackers and cyber thieves to steal data or to do some harmful actions on a user's computer or network.
- Unlike worms, Trojan horses do not replicate themselves.

Spyware

- It is a malicious program that installs itself on a user's computer without his consent and collects sensitive information, internet usage, online behavior, etc., Unlike Trojan, its purpose is not to control the user's computer but to monitor the online behavior and activities to collect data for commercial use.
- It observes the online activities of the user and sent them to the snooper.
- Spyware is mainly used by hackers, business firms, e-commerce sites, marketing organizations, etc.

Adware

- Adware is malware that pops up unwanted advertisements on a computer screen.
- These ads are possibly targeted to the interests of the users by using information collected by spyware.

Ransomware

- Ransomware is malicious software that infects a user's computer system and displays messages demanding a fee to be paid to use the system again.

- It is criminal money-making malware. It can lock the computer or encrypt files to demand money.

How do avoid or remove Malware?

Install Anti-virus/Anti-malware program

- Anti-virus is software that can be used to remove malware such as viruses from the computer system.
- Install a trusted Anti-virus, anti-malware, and internet security software (such as Kaspersky, Norton, Avira, K7, etc.) and keep this software updated regularly.

Install software from reliable sources only

- Install software from reliable sources such as Google Play store, Microsoft store, software center of Linux, App Store of Apple, direct websites of software companies, etc.

Use/Install firewall

- Firewall is a hardware component or software that monitors incoming and outgoing network traffic and blocks malware and unauthorized entries.
- Firewall ranges from basic software such as windows defender to specialized network security devices.

Use a genuine operating system and keep it updated

- Do not use a pirated operating system on your computer.
- Use the genuine operating system and keep it updated.

Testing in a single computer: Test new devices, applications, etc., in a single computer that is secured with anti-virus/internet security software.

Secure networks: Secure your Wi-Fi networks with strong passwords and other measures. Never use unsecured networks such as public Wi-Fi, Wi-Fi hotspots, etc., to share data.

Think before clicking: Do not open email attachments from unknown sources. Never click on links in unsolicited email and WhatsApp messages.

Back up data regularly: It is important to back up data regularly on external devices or cloud storage.

3.

Ethical Issues (Cyber Ethics)

- Cyberethics refers to a code of safe and responsible behavior of the internet community.
- Cyberethics is the moral, legal, and ethical values to be followed by the users of computers and the internet.
- It must be communicated to the students, managers, employees, and other internet users.
- Cyberethics is now incorporated as part of corporate policies. Many companies are now giving compulsory training on cyberethics to their employees.

Cyber Ethics

Examples of practices that violate cyberethics are

- Plagiarism: Copying the work of others and using it as own.
- Software Piracy: Unauthorised duplication and use of software
- Collect & use the data of the internet community without their consent etc.
- Use online customer data in a manner affecting their privacy

4. Information Overload

- Too much information presented before a person makes it difficult
  for him to find out which is relevant and which is irrelevant.
- Information overload refers to the difficulty in understanding an issue and making a decision because of the availability of too much
  information.
- Technically, Information overload occurs when the amount of input
  to a system exceeds its processing capacity.
- Information Overload is an increasing problem both in the workplace & in life. (especially for direction, managers & professionals)
- Example: Getting too many e-mails, reports, letters, and messages
  in a business. It creates problems to decide what is important and
  unimportant.

Causes of Information Overload

1. Multiple sources of information

- If the data is collected from multiple sources, it leads to duplication of data and information overload.

2. Lack of information processing capacity of the people:

- Capacity of a person to process information is influenced by education, experience, training, etc.

3. Development of computer technology:

- The availability of too much information is the result of the development of computer technology and

4. Poor mechanism to handle data in the organization

- If the organization is not well equipped to handle data, it creates information overload.

5. Limited availability of time

- Limited time available to process information may crate information overload.

6. Complex processes and tasks

- To perform complex processes and tasks, more information may be required and the same may lead to information overload.

How to solve information overload?

- **Filter data:** Focus attention on most essential information and ignore the other.
- **Multi-tasking:** perform two or more jobs at the same time
- **Priorities tasks:** Arrange tasks based on importance and take the most important ones first.
- **Delegate works:** Delegate some works to sub-ordinates. Instructions may be given to send related communication to the respective sub-ordinate.
- **Delete after reading:** Delete unwanted information immediately after reading.
- **Adopt technology:** Use technology to process and visualize the data.

How to solve information overload?

- **Use personal devices:** Use personal notebooks, tabs, etc.., to store
  organized data.

- **Hire secretaries:** Hire well-trained secretaries or assistants to help
  with the management of data.
- **Unsubscribe periodicals:** Cancel email subscription of unwanted
  periodicals by clicking the link to unsubscribe.
- **Request to clients:** Request all clients to send important messages only and to avoid messages of minor importance.
- **Restrict email:** Send email on important matters only.
- **Alter the way of doing a task:** Try to do the task in different ways.
  Example: Take a printout and read instead of reading on a computer
  screen, work outside the office, etc.

5. Cyber Crime & Cyber security

- Cybercrime is a crime that involves a computer and network.
- It is the crime that either target a computer or committed through an electronic device or computer network.
- Cybercrimes are defined as "Offences that are committed with a criminal motive using modern telecommunication networks such as the Internet and mobile phones"

- Cybercriminals may be children and adolescents, black hat hackers, discontented employees, terrorists, etc.

1. Identity Theft:

- It is the crime of obtaining or stealing the personal or financial information of another person to use for personal gain.
- It may be used to commit frauds, obtain loans, make cellular connections, make unauthorized transactions, etc.

2. Hacking

- It refers to gaining or accessing one's computer system or network without permission.
- It is unauthorized entry into a computer or network to steal data, change information, or damage the system.
- A hacker is a criminal who accesses someone else 's computer without permission.

White hat hackers and Black hat hackers

- "White hats" are good and ethical hackers and the "Black hats" are criminals.
- White hat hackers are security experts who try to find the vulnerabilities in programs and systems and report them to the manufacturers.
- Companies such as Google and Apple are offering rewards of a million dollars to white hat hackers who can find defects in their security systems.
- Black hat hackers are criminals who attack computers and networks with bad intentions.

3. E-mailing:

- It is the process of sending huge volumes of e-mail to a target address to overflow the mailbox.
- It may lead to server overload, server failure, information overload, etc.
- Some types of these emails can be detected by using spam filters.

4. Phishing:

- It is a fraudulent attempt to collect sensitive information such as debit card number, username, password, etc. through email, telephone or other means.
- The bank and other authorities never send messages to their customers asking for this kind of information. Never reply to such
  email, SMS, and telephone calls.

5. Child Pornography

- It is the visual depiction of sexually explicit content involving a child.
- Creating, uploading, watching, downloading, or spreading nude pictures and videos of a person who is under 18 years of age is child pornography.
- It is a criminal offense in India and liable to fine and imprisonment (IT Act 2000 and POCSO act2012)

6. Malware attack

- It is the attack of cybercriminals by using malware.
- Malware such as viruses, Trojan horses, spyware, etc., are created and sent to target computers to cause damage to the system or network.
- Ransomware is also used by criminals to block the system and demand money.

7. Spoofing

- Spoofing is the act of disguising a communication from an unknown source claiming that it is from a known and trusted source. Eg. E-mail spoofing, URL spoofing.

8. Denial of services (DoS):

- It means to shut down a computer, website, or network making it inaccessible to its intended users.

9. Salami Attack

- Salami attack is a series of minor attacks that together result in a larger attack and serious damage.

Cyber Security (How to prevent Cyber Crime?)

Cyber security is the technology and practices designed to protect computers and networks from malware and cybercrimes. Following are the main cyber security measures.

- Install Anti-virus, firewall, and internet security software in the computer system.
- Use a genuine operating system and software and update it regularly.
- Use strong passwords and change them regularly.
- securely manage your social media settings.

Cyber Security (How to prevent Cyber Crime?)

- Strengthen the security of the home network.

- Use encryption, encoding, etc.., while sending

strategic data online.

- Don't disclose sensitive information to anyone through calls, SMS, email, and other

communications.

- Keep an eye on kids who spent time online.
- Know what to do if you become a victim.

5. Cyber Addiction

- Cyber addiction is the excessive and non-productive use of computers, smart, phones, and the internet.
- It is the excessive use of electronic devices that interferes with daily life, work, and relationship.
- It involves the excessive use of social media, involvement in online gambling, online game addiction, cybersex addiction, etc.
- Cyber addiction affects our psychological functioning, mental health, and general well-being.

Signs and symptoms of Cyber addiction

- Using of computer or mobile phone (Internet) longer than intended
- Unable to work because of online activity.
- Isolation from family and friends because of spending much online
- Feeling guilty or defensive about your internet use
- Use the internet to escape from worries & tension.
- Physical symptoms- dry eyes, backaches, etc.

- More online friends than real-life friends.
- Losing sleep, neglecting studies, little food, etc.

How to manage Cyber addiction

- **Self-control:** Set time and limit for internet usage.
- Identify the underlying reason: Try to identify the underlying reason that leads to cyber addiction.
- **Increase coping skills:** Ask support of friends, create a to-do list, engage in good activities, walk away from stressful situations, etc.
- **Strengthen relationships**- with friends, family members, etc.
- Identify and uninstall addictive apps.

Towards Child or Teenagers

- Place the computer in the common room
- Monitor computer/ Mobile phone use
- Encourage other interests, hobbies & social activities
- Talk to the child about underlying issues.
- Arrange a counseling session if strongly addicted.

Electronic Waste (E-WASTE)

- E-waste means all waste caused by discarded electronic & electrical devices.
- It refers to all items of electrical and electronic equipment (EEE) and their pasts that have been discarded by their owners as waste.

- E-waste is mainly created by discarded electronic devices such as computers, laptops, mobile phones, tablets, DVD players, television, etc.
- E-waste has turned out to be a serious environmental issue for many nations.
- E-waste is a major concern in the area of personal computing because wireless devices are quickly discarded by consumers.
- Consumers generally buy new instead of reusing because their electronic devices quickly become obsolete or it may be cheaper to purchase new.
- Electronic equipment is manufactured using numerous toxic contents and harmful components.
- Informal processing of electronic waste in developing & underdeveloped countries may cause serious health and pollution problems.

E-waste Management in Various Countries

- Most developed countries have taken measures to control e-waste. WHO has also addressed this issue & specified guidelines.
- Basel Convention, is an international treaty that was designed to reduce the movement of hazardous waste between nations, specifically from developed countries.
- Waste Electronic & Electronic (WEEE) Regulation is a directive in the European Union that designates safe and responsible collection, recycling, and recovery procedures for all types of electronic waste.
- Most developing & underdeveloped countries are yet to take concrete steps to manage e-waste.

Impacts of E-waste

Environmental Impact

- Air, water, and soil pollution
- Affects plants & animals.
- Human health issues created by the toxic content of dumpede-waste.

Economic Impact

- Substantial public spending on health care
- Investment in collection & recycling
- Wastage of resources
- Opportunities for recycling industries. (Positive impact)

How to manage E-waste?

Responsibilities of Industries

- **Inventory management**- Reduce hazardous materials used in the production of electronic devices.
- **Changes in the production process-** Correct handling & operating procedures, proper maintenance of machines, etc.
- **Eco-friendly product design-** Design products that can be made up of non-toxic materials which are reusable & recyclable.
- Adopt Green Computing standards (see next topic)
- **Collections and recycling**- There must be facilities to recollect damaged devices and recycle them.

Responsibilities of Citizens or Users

- **Repair and reuse**-Repair and reuse devices maximum as possible.
- **Exchange:** Exchange old devices while buying new devices.
- **Avoid Dumping:** Avoid dumping waste in soil and water. Don't try to burn e-waste.
- **Green disposal of waste:** Make arrangements to bring waste into recycling centers.
- **Donating electronics for reuse**- Donate devices to ready persons & organizations.

Responsibilities of the Government

- **Proper education about the danger of e-waste**- Proper education and awareness must be given to the producers and users about the danger of e-waste.
- **Heavy fine for industries**- which do not practice waste prevention & green computing.
- **Collection and recycling**- There must be facilities to collect and recycle discarded devices.
- **Laws and Regulations:** E-waste must be controlled through proper laws and regulations by the Government.

Green Computing

- It is the study and practice of designing, manufacturing, using, and disposing of computers and other electronic devices efficiently and effectively with minimal or no impact on the environment
- The goals of green computing are
- To reduce the use of hazardous materials
- To maximize energy efficiency during the product's lifetime

- To promote the recyclability of defunct products and factory waste.

Components of Green computing

- **Green design**- Designing energy-efficient, environmentally friendly products
- **Green manufacturing**- Manufacturing devices with less hazardous components
- **Green use**- Maximum use, save energy
- **Green disposal**- Reusing, proper recycling

Health Issues

- A large percentage of our daily life is spent with a personal computer, laptop, tablet, smartphone, etc.
- Constant technology usage can create many health problems, both physical and emotional.
- **Physical:** Stress in eyes, Finger pain, back pain, headaches, weight gain or loss, disturbances in sleep
- **Mental or emotional:** Impatience, fatigue, depression, isolation, defensiveness, etc.

Guidelines for proper usage of Computers and the Internet

Health Guidelines

- Maintain good sitting posture when working at a computer. Utilize a chair with back support.
- Avoid hitting the keyboard with excessive force.
- Rest your eyes by refocusing on distant objects intermittently when working.
- Position the monitor centered directly in front of you so that your neck is in a neutral or straight position. The top of the computer screen should be slightly below the top of your head.
- Ensure break in between continuous use- get up, move around, and do an alternative activity
- Ensure adequate lighting in the room.

Operational & Ethical Guidelines

- Respect for copyright materials. Avoid plagiarism.
- Use genuine operating system and software
- Use the internet mainly for education and communication purposes- searching for knowledge, email, preparation of assignments, etc.
- Chose strong passwords for accounts.
- Back up the data regularly
- Never disclose personal information to strangers.
- Avoid unsolicited mail and other communications
- Use firewall and anti-virus software to prevent malware attacks
- Proper shut down after use
- Use energy-saving instruments
- Re-use electronic devices as possible
- Avoid unauthorized/unsecured websites

Cyberspace: Issues and Threats

- Privacy and security of data.
- Malware- such as Computer Virus
- Ethical Issues (Cyberethics)
- Cybercrime & cyber security
- Information overload
- Cyber addiction
- Health issues
- E-waste & Green computing etc.

Cyber Laws in India

- Cyberlaw is part of the overall legal system that deals with cyberspace regulation and security.
- There is no dedicated cyber security law in India. But the Information Technology Act 2000 (IT Act) contains a provision regarding the regulation of cybercrimes.
- The main purpose of the act is to provide legal recognition for electronic transactions.
- However, section 65-78 of the act specifically deals with offenses that come under cybercrimes.

IT ACT 2000

- The UNICITRAL Model Law on International Commercial Arbitration was passed in 1985 and the United Nations General Assembly has adopted the Model Law.
- The model law is not binding, but countries may adopt the provisions of the law by incorporating it into their domestic laws.
- Following the UN Resolution, India passed the Information Technology Act 2000 which incorporated the provision of the

model law. It was amended in 2008.

- The act applies to the whole of India. It also applied for offenses committed outside India which involve computer resources in India.
- Some of the main issues addressed by the Information Technology Act are;

- Legal Recognition of Electronic Documents (e-Governance)
- Legal Recognition of Digital Signatures-in place of a written signature
- Offences come under cybercrimes.
- Penalties and compensations

Offenses & Penalties (Section 65 to 78 of the Act)

Offences & Penalties (Section 65 to 78 of the IT Act)			
Section	**Offence**	**Imprisonment Up to**	**Fine Up to**
65	**Conceal, destroy or alter computer source documents**	**3 Years**	**2 Lakhs**
66A	**Sending Offensive messages**	**3 Years**	**5 Lakhs**
66B	**Dishonestly receiving stolen computer or communication devices**	**3 Years**	**1 Lakh**
66C	**Identity theft**	**3 Years**	**2 Lakhs**
66D	**Cheating by personation by using computer resource**	**3 years**	**1 Lakh**
66E	**Violation of privacy**	**3 Years**	**2 Lakhs**
66F	**Cyber terrorism**	**For life**	**5 Lakhs**

Offenses & Penalties

Section	Offence	Imprisonment Up to	Fine Up to
67	Publishing or transmitting obscene materials in electronic form	3/5 years	5/10 Lakhs
67A	Publishing or transmitting sexually explicit content	5/7 Years	10 Lakhs
67B	Publishing or transmitting sexually explicit content depicting children	5/7 Years	10 Lakhs
71	Misrepresentation of material fact with controller or certifying authority	2 Years	1 Lakhs
72	Breach of confidentiality and privacy	2 Years	1 Lakh
72 A	Disclosure of information in breach of lawful contract	3 Years	5 Lakhs
73	Publishing false certificates	2 years	1 Lakh

Offenses & Penalties

Electronic Governance (e-Governance)

- It is the application of Information technology in Government functioning and for the delivery of Government services.
- It is the integration of ICT at all levels of the Government for better governance.
- It involves the use of ICT by the Government to:
- Exchange of information with a citizen, businesses, and other agencies
- Improving efficiency
- Reducing cost and delay
- Restricting administration processes
- Improving quality of services

Stages of e-Governance

- Computerisation of Government offices and departments

- Networking of all Government organizations
- Online presence- An active, secure, and well-maintained website that contains all information.
- Online interactivity- There must be facilities for the public to interact with Govt. through websites. Example: Online submission of forms, facility to download, complaint, queries, online file tracking, etc.
- e-infrastructure, e-literacy to citizens/ sufficient e-Seva centers

Types of Interactions in e-Governance

- **G 2 G (Govt. to Govt.):** Information communication and interactions within and between government entities such as state government, central government, and local governments.
- **G 2 C (Govt. to Citizen):** Efficient delivery of Government services to the citizen by electronic means.
- **G 2 B (Govt. to Business):** Electronic communications & interactions between business and government such as licensing, permit, tax collection, etc.
- **G 2 E (Govt. to Employees):** Efficient interaction with employees such as circulation of information, salary processing, reports, etc.

Benefits of e-Governance

- It makes the Government closer to citizen
- Simplicities of the process of information exchange
- Better delivery of quality services to the citizen & businesses.
- Transparency in Government administration.
- Automation of Government services
- Elimination of Corruption in Government entities

- Any time, anywhere availability of information & services
- Improved interaction with business and employees
- Reduction in cost, better management, greater convenience, revenue growth, etc.

e-Governance Initiates in India

- **National e-Governance Plan:** Formulated by the Department of Electronics and Information Technology – aims at improving the delivery of government services to citizens. It consists of 27 missing mode projects which is the base of all e-governance initiates.
- **My Gov-** Websites and applications launched by the Government of India (G2C) to ensure active participation of the citizen in Government.
- **Digital India:** Digital India is a program of the Government of India with a vision to transform India into a digitally empowered society and knowledge economy.
- **UDAI:** Unique Identification Authority of India was created to issue Unique Identification numbers (UID), named "Aadhaar", to all residents of India.
- **Direct Benefits Transfer (DBT):** A program of the Government of India to transfer subsidies directly to the bank account of beneficiaries.
- **Aadhar enabled payment system (AEPS):** It is a system developed by NPC to make Aadhar-based cash withdrawals, transfers, and other payments through micro ATMs.
- **IRCTC/IRCTC Rail Connect (G2C):** It is the online & mobile platform for train ticket reservation of India Railway.
- **Passport Seva (G2C):** Online platform for the delivery of passport services to the citizen through Passport Seva Kendras.
- **Immigration, Visa, and Foreigner's registration and Tracking (IVFRT):** Online platform for immigration, Visa, and related

services to the international travelers.

- **Mobile Seva:** It is an initiative aimed at implementing mobile governance in the country
- **e-procurement (G2B):** It is a system that enables business firms to submit online bids for government purchases.
- **BHIM UPI:** It is an initiative to enable fast, secure, reliable cashless, payments through mobile phones.
- **DIGILOCKER:** A mobile document wallet that allows a citizen to keep their documents in approved

CHAPTER FIVE

Digital Marketing

What is Digital Marketing?

- Digital marketing has become one of the most popular mantras in the last couple of years.
- Development of digital technologies brought about a fast and systematic shift from traditional marketing to digital marketing.
- Digital marketing is the marketing through digital or electronic media.
- Digital marketing is any form of marketing that involves electronic devices.
- In digital marketing, digital media and internet resources are utilized to reach consumers.
- It can be done both online & offline

Factors contributed to the growth of Digital Marketing

- Increased use of smartphones
- Popularity of the internet
- Low internet charges
- Improved connectivity (Broadband, 4G, 5G, etc.)

- Social Media revolution
- Advancement in Television transmission (D2H, smart TVs, etc.)
- Growth of e-Commerce

Meaning and Concept of Digital Marketing

- Computerized advertising alludes to the showcasing of items, administrations, and thoughts that use advanced innovations and the web.
- Digital advertising is an expansive term that incorporates all advanced showcasing stations and techniques (web, TV, cell phones, and so on) that can be utilized to advance items or administrations.
- Digital showcasing uses the extent of a web crawler, email, web-based entertainment, TV, cell phones, visual advancements, and so forth.

Difference between Traditional Marketing & Digital Marketing

Traditional Marketing	Digital Marketing
Domination of print media	**Domination of electronic media**
Less Interactivity	**More Interactivity**
Time consuming (delayed)	**Fast and efficient (immediate)**
Costly	**Cost effective**
Low coverage	**Huge coverage (all over the globe)**
Limited audience	**Reach out to maximum people**
Difficult to measure the result	**Measurable & real time result**
Not available always	**Available always (24 x 7 days)**

Difference between Traditional Marketing & Digital Marketing

Need/Importance/Advantages of Digital Marketing

- **Cost-effective**: Digital promotion is more affordable and more powerful than customary advertising.
- **Mobile access-:** It can be gotten to through cell phones.
- **Flexibility;** There are various sorts of types of advanced advertising instruments reasonable to different items, administrations, and circumstances.
- **Interactivity**-It permits intelligence with clients
- **Coverage** — Wide region (all around the globe) can be covered.
- **More extensive reach** — It contacts the greatest individuals
- **Personalisation** — Digital showcasing assists with customizing the substance of advancement.
- **Brand notoriety** It is useful to rapidly construct the brand.
- **Increased income** — Digital showcasing gives more deals and income.
- **Measurable** — It is not difficult to track and screen the computerized promoting adequacy. •
- **Meet Competition** — It permits all organizations to contend with enormous enterprises and MNCs.

Weaknesses of Digital Marketing

- **Dependence on the web** — The Internet isn't open in specific regions. Not every person utilizes the web routinely.
- **High contest** — The organizations utilizing computerized advertising need to contend with a huge measure of organizations all around the globe.

- **Not appropriate for all classifications of items:** It is reasonable to explicit classifications of items as it were. For instance: it may not be reasonable to modern merchandise, drug items, and so on.
- **Protection and security**: Digital promotion is dependent upon protection and security issues. There are chances of digital assaults on sites and other promoting channels.
- **Complaints and inputs:** Bad surveys, negative remarks, inability to answer, and so on, can harm brand notoriety.
- **No private communication**: Digital promotion doesn't permit the eye to eye association.

Business models in digital marketing

The business market is gigantic because a higher extent of firms is associated with the Internet than customers, particularly in non-industrial nations. Advertisers who handle what Internet advancements can improve are ready to exploit data innovation.

1) Business to Business (B2B)

Business-to-business - "B2B" - alludes to trade between two organizations instead of to business between a business and a singular customer. Exchanges at the discount level are business-to-business. In straightforward, it alludes to any advertising technique or content that is equipped towards

a business or association. Any organization that sells items or then again administrations to different organizations or associations (versus purchasers) ordinarily utilizes B2B showcasing procedures.

2) Business to Customer (B2C)

B2C is an abbreviation for "business-to-purchaser." A B2C business sells items or administrations straightforwardly to the buyer. With the capacity to sell straightforwardly to buyers, the B2C model, fundamentally, disposed of the agent and, frequently times disposes of the requirement for eBay, Amazon, and others completely. The test of the business-to-shopper model is that organizations need to keep a consistent deals steam to remain practical. At the point when the economy gets intense, customers may make changes in their spending, and that can influence a B2C business.

3) Client to Customer (C2C)

C2C, client to client, or purchaser to the customer, is a plan of action that works with the exchange of items or on the other hand benefits between clients. Buyer to the shopper, or C2C is the plan of action that works with business between private people. Whether it's for merchandise or administration, this class of web-based business interfaces individuals to work with each other.

4) Business to Employees (B2E)

A methodology wherein the focal point of business is the representative, instead of the shopper (for all intents and purposes in business-to-customer, or B2C) or different organizations (for what it's worth in business-to-business or B2B). The B2E approach outgrew the continuous lack of data innovation (IT) laborers. From a wide perspective, B2E incorporates all that organizations do to draw in and hold capable staff in a serious market, for example, forceful enrolling strategies, benefits, instruction potential open doors, adaptable hours, rewards, what's more, worker strengthening methodologies.

5) Business to Government (B2G)

A plan of action that alludes to organizations selling items, administrations, or data to legislatures or government offices. B2G organizations or models give an approach to organizations to offer on government activities or items that legislatures could buy or need for their associations. This can include public area associations that propose the offers. B2G exercises are progressively being directed using the Internet through the real-time offering.

Printed by Libri Plureos GmbH in Hamburg,
Germany